THE NEGRO IN CONGRESS
1870-1901

THE

NEGRO

IN

CONGRESS

1870-1901

SAMUEL DENNY SMITH, Ph.D.

Associate Professor of Social Studies

MISSISSIPPI STATE COLLEGE FOR WOMEN

KENNIKAT PRESS, INC./PORT WASHINGTON, N. Y.

TO

SAMUEL DENNY, JUNIOR

AND

DORRIS ANN

FOREWORD

BY

J. G. DE ROULHAC HAMILTON

DURING THE PAST FORTY YEARS that period of American history so inaccurately called Reconstruction has been a subject of investigation by a large number of historical writers, who, basing their studies on original sources, have painted quite a different picture from that one widely accepted outside the South. The latter had for its basis chiefly political propaganda and the prejudiced recollections and reminiscences of active and partisan participants in the bitter political struggle following upon the Civil War, a struggle which seemed likely to justify General Winfield Scott's anguished prophecy that it would "take several generations and all the conservatism of the nation to quell the fury of the non-combatants—after the war is over." This literature is of a sort that might be expected. Its chief value is to be found in the light it throws upon the state of mind of the aforesaid actors on the public stage.

The impetus which started the new movement was furnished chiefly by that accomplished investigator and great teacher, William A. Dunning. His own two very important contributions to the history of the period pointed the way, and under his enthusiastic guidance studies of Reconstruction were made for a majority of the lately seceded states, and doubtless led to similar ones for several others.

Additional stimulus was given to the movement by the publication of several notable original sources hitherto inaccessible, the most important being the diary of Gideon Welles. In large measure these justified the findings and conclusions of the investigators. Presently biography aided by its new and realistic portraiture of various important figures. Andrew Johnson received a long-delayed vindication. Sumner and Stevens and a host of minor deities descended from seats among the gods and took on the guise of mere frail mortals, so much so, indeed, as to arouse in many minds doubts as to the accuracy of the generally accepted belief that dead politicians are statesmen. A generation removed from the passions of the civil war and its aftermath looked upon the work and found it good, and presently a considerable number of popular books on the period diffused the findings of the historical group and made their story the one generally accepted by the reading public. Today it is difficult to find among intelligent and informed people a defender of the congressional policy of Reconstruction.

It might seem from this that the whole story had been told, but that is not the case. Apart from the fact that a historical story is never complete, and that each generation will interpret and write history in its own terms, the history of the Reconstruction, as written, still lacks completeness. There are still a great many phases of it which require investigation.

Dr. Smith's study is a fine example of the investigation of such an important phase and is one of the first to be undertaken. With careful and extensive use of all available sources, with balanced judgment, he has studied the lives and careers of an interesting group of men, who, under no other conditions than those which prevailed in the South at the time, would ever have been found in the Congress of the United States. That South Carolina should be governed by recent laborers in its rice fields, and in the way so vividly portrayed by Pike in *The Prostrate State,* was no more remarkable than that Jefferson Davis should be succeeded in the Senate by

Hiram Revels. Each fact excited thrilled approval in the North. The facts behind the fervid approval of the first have been clearly described in the more general studies of the period; Dr. Smith has shown clearly how little justification there was for it so far as the presence of the Negro in the hall of Congress was concerned. He has done so in an unbiased and scholarly fashion, and has pointed the way to new fields of investigation.

Chapel Hill, North Carolina.
January 25th, 1940

PREFACE

THIS STUDY IS A SURVEY of the careers of all Negroes who served in Congress during the period of 1870-1901 and an attempt to evaluate their achievements. Some few unsuccessful Negro candidates for Congress have been considered important enough to be given consideration.

Documentary research for this study has been augmented by interviews with Negro leaders to obtain their opinions of their political pioneers. Three Negro ex-congressmen were living until recently; one was interviewed in person, the others by letter. All have died since then.

For the reader's convenience, tables have been compiled citing Negro percentages of population in counties and states, number of Negroes in all Congresses of the period, the racial stock of these congressmen, their education, previous professions, and social status before the Civil War.

It should be noticed that no attempt has been made to include the careers of the Negroes who have served in Congress in recent years. That is quite a different story; also, the participants are still active, and it would be impossible to pass final judgment on them.

This study was undertaken at the suggestion of Dr. J. G. de R. Hamilton of The University of North Carolina, and he gave valuable advice and assistance in the research and in the putting together of the material. To my wife, Mabel Dorris Smith, I wish to acknowledge my indebtedness for her encouragement and for her typing of the manuscript.

SAMUEL DENNY SMITH

Columbus, Mississippi
1940

CONTENTS

THE NEGRO IN CONGRESS
1870-1901

I

INTRODUCTION

By 1870 CONGRESSIONAL RECONSTRUCTION was in full sway in the South, the Fourteenth Amendment was in effect, and the local and state governments of the seceding states were, to a large extent, in the hands of Negroes. During 1870 the Fifteenth Amendment became effective, and the last of the seceding states was readmitted to the union. Negroes had been elected to the state offices of lieutenant-governor, Speaker of the House, Secretary of State, state auditor, state superintendent of education, and justice of a state supreme court. Negroes acted as governors in Mississippi and Louisiana. Therefore, it was natural that Negroes should aspire to federal elective offices. From time to time it will be necessary to refer to state and local politics in order to understand the backgrounds of the Negroes who were elected to Congress.

The massing of Negroes in the so-called "Black Belts" was even more evident in 1870 than it is today, and it was this section which furnished all the Negro congressmen in the period to be considered. However, the census of 1870 was defective in regard to the Negro population. It was supposed that 500,000 Negroes in the South were uncounted in this census.[1] The census of 1890 also showed an

[1] *Negro Population in the United States 1890-1915*, Samuel L. Rogers, Director, pp. 26, 208.

undercount of Negroes.[2] Therefore, for our purpose the census of 1880 will give the most accurate information concerning the Negro sections of the South; that date corresponds fairly well to the time when the most Negroes were serving in Congress.

A study of the racial divisions in the eleven seceding states will make it clear why the Negro congressmen were all elected from eight of these states and why none were elected from Texas, Arkansas, or Tennessee. The Negro element in the other former slave states, namely, Kentucky, Maryland, Missouri, and Delaware, was so small as to have no political influence apart from that of the white Republicans of those states. Of the eight states from which Negroes were elected to Congress none ever had more than one Negro congressman at one time, with the exceptions of South Carolina and Mississippi. South Carolina had four of them in the House at the same time, and Mississippi had a senator and a representative at the same time.

Figures from the 1880 census are given in the following table: [3]

STATE	WHITES	NEGROES	NEGRO PERCENTAGE
Virginia	880,858	631,616	41.8
North Carolina	867,242	531,277	37.9
South Carolina	391,105	604,332	60.7
Georgia	816,906	725,133	47
Florida	142,605	126,690	47
Tennessee	1,138,831	403,151	26.2
Alabama	662,185	600,103	47.5
Mississippi	479,398	650,291	57.5
Arkansas	591,531	210,666	26.3
Louisiana	454,954	483,655	51.5
Texas	1,197,237	393,384	24.7

[2] *Ibid.*, p. 27.
[3] *Ibid.*, pp. 26, 208.

When the statistics for sections and counties are examined, the Negro concentration is found to be even more marked. This concentration was usually in the coastal region, but there are exceptions. The boundaries of the black districts were changed from time to time, and we cannot identify them throughout the period by the same counties. Yet they remained essentially the same: [4] the central district in Georgia, the northern in Florida, the western in Mississippi, the south central in Alabama, the east central in Louisiana, the eastern in North Carolina, and the southeastern in Virginia. In spite of gerrymandering, certain counties were always included in the black districts, and it is instructive to notice some of them:

CENSUS OF 1880 [5]

STATE	COUNTY	NEGRO PERCENTAGE
Virginia	Amelia	70.7
"	Prince Edward	67.6
North Carolina	Edgecombe	69.6
" "	Craven	66.2
" "	Halifax	69.8
South Carolina	Aiken	54.0
" "	Charleston	69.9
" "	Georgetown	82.3
" "	Beaufort	91.9
" "	Sumter	73.1
Georgia	Burke	77.5
"	Lee	83.5
Alabama	Dallas	82.6
"	Greene	82.8
"	Lowndes	81.9

[4] *Ibid.*
[5] *Ibid.*, pp. 776-793.

CENSUS OF 1880

STATE	COUNTY	NEGRO PERCENTAGE
Florida	Alachua	60.8
Mississippi	Bolivar	85.6
"	Washington	86.2
"	Adams	78.8
"	Tunica	91.7
"	Sharkey	77.6
"	Coahoma	82.2
Louisiana	Tensas	91.1
"	East Carroll	91.4
"	Madison	90.9

The significance of these overwhelmingly Negro percentages becomes apparent when we see how one of the Negro congressmen, "boss" in his home county, is able thereby to swing the district convention to his own nomination. Also we shall see, in each state separately, how the whites bitterly resented this condition and strove to overcome the Negro majorities, either by legal methods of redistricting and of qualifying suffrage, or by illegal methods of violence, fraud, and intimidation. However, even when the whites controlled the state as a whole, they still had a long fight to regain control of all congressional districts, and the century was closing before the last Negro was ousted from Congress.

In the period under survey twenty-two Negroes served in Congress: twenty in the House of Representatives, and two in the Senate. A number of others claimed to have been elected, and about thirty were unsuccessful candidates.[6] Both the senators were from Mississippi. The representatives were distributed as follows: eight from South Carolina; four from North Carolina; three from Alabama; and one each from

[6] Special attention will be given these candidates in Chap. V.

Virginia, Georgia, Florida, Louisiana, and Mississippi. There was at least one Negro in every Congress from the Forty-first to the Fifty-sixth inclusive, with the exception of the Fiftieth. The twenty-two Negroes served a total of seven years in the Senate and sixty-four in the House, or seventy-one in all. Neither senator was re-elected, but ten, or exactly half, of the representatives were. The following table shows the distribution in the different Congresses.[7]

NUMBER OF CONGRESS	DATE	MEMBER	STATE	TOTAL MEMBERSHIP
41	1869-71	J. H. Rainey	South Carolina	
		J. F. Long	Georgia	
		* H. R. Revels	Mississippi	3
42	1871-73	J. T. Walls	Florida	
		B. S. Turner	Alabama	
		J. H. Rainey	South Carolina	
		R. C. DeLarge	South Carolina	
		R. B. Elliott	South Carolina	5
43	1873-75	R. B. Elliott	South Carolina	
		R. H. Cain	South Carolina	
		A. J. Ransier	South Carolina	
		J. H. Rainey	South Carolina	
		J. T. Rapier	Alabama	
		J. T. Walls	Florida	
		J. R. Lynch	Mississippi	7
44	1875-77	J. R. Lynch	Mississippi	
		* B. K. Bruce	Mississippi	
		J. T. Walls	Florida	

[7] *Biographical Congressional Directory 1774-1927, passim* (hereinafter cited *Cong. Directory*); *Negro Year Book*, 1921-1922, ed. Monroe N. Work, pp. 243 f.

Oscar DePriest served in the Seventy-first and Seventy-second Congresses; Arthur Mitchell in the Seventy-third through Seventy-sixth Congresses. Both served the First Illinois District, DePriest as a Republican and Mitchell as a New Deal Democrat. Their careers do not fall within the scope of this book.

NUMBER OF CONGRESS	DATE	MEMBER	STATE	TOTAL MEMBERSHIP
		Jeremiah Haralson	Alabama	
		J. A. Hyman	North Carolina	
		C. E. Nash	Louisiana	
		J. H. Rainey	South Carolina	
		R. Smalls	South Carolina	8
45	1877-79	R. H. Cain	South Carolina	
		J. H. Rainey	South Carolina	
		R. Smalls	South Carolina	
		* B. K. Bruce	Mississippi	4
46	1879-81	* B. K. Bruce	Mississippi	1
47	1881-83	R. Smalls	South Carolina	
		J. R. Lynch	Mississippi	2
48	1883-85	J. E. O'Hara	North Carolina	
		R. Smalls	South Carolina	2
49	1885-87	R. Smalls	South Carolina	
		J. E. O'Hara	North Carolina	2
51	1889-91	H. P. Cheatham	North Carolina	
		T. E. Miller	South Carolina	
		J. M. Langston	Virginia	3
52	1891-93	H. P. Cheatham	North Carolina	1
53	1893-95	G. W. Murray	South Carolina	1
54	1895-97	G. W. Murray	South Carolina	1
55	1897-99	G. H. White	North Carolina	1
56	1899-1901	G. H. White	North Carolina	1

* Member of Senate.

In considering their fitness for the positions they held, I have prepared some classifications as to racial stock, education, profession, and previous social condition of these men, without at this place going into a discussion of the significance of these factors.

RACIAL STOCK

PURE NEGRO BLOOD	MIXED BLOOD	
Cain	Cheatham	Miller
Haralson	DeLarge	Nash
Murray	Hyman	O'Hara
Elliott [8]	Langston	Rainey
	Lynch	Ransier
	Long	Rapier
	Smalls	Turner
	Walls	White
	Bruce	Revels

EDUCATION

COLLEGE TRAINING		SECONDARY SCHOOL TRAINING OR LESS	
Cain	Miller (Graduate)	Rainey	Smalls
O'Hara	Cheatham (Graduate)	Hyman	DeLarge
Bruce	Langston (Graduate)	Lynch	Rapier
Murray	Elliott (Graduate)	Nash	Haralson
Revels	White (Graduate)	Ransier	Turner
		Long	Walls

Woodson claims that most Negro congressmen had more formal education than Warren G. Harding.[9] This claim may be questioned, for Harding attended college for three years.[10]

---

[8] Edward B. Reuter, *The Mulatto in the United States*, p. 251, gives this division except for Elliott, whom he classifies as a mulatto. In Chap. III I shall submit contemporary opinion that he was of pure Negro blood.

[9] Carter G. Woodson, *The Negro in Our History*, p. 406; *Cong. Directory*, *passim*.

[10] *World Almanac*, 1928, p. 240.

PROFESSIONS [11]

LAWYERS	PREACHERS	FARMERS	PUBLIC OFFICIALS
Langston	Cain	Hyman	Cheatham
Miller	Haralson	DeLarge	Bruce
Elliott	Revels	Walls	
White		Rapier	
O'Hara			
Lynch			

BARBER	BRICKLAYER	TEACHER	TAILOR
Rainey	Nash	Murray	Long

SHIPPING CLERK	PILOT	LIVERYMAN
Ransier	Smalls	Turner

PREVIOUS SOCIAL STATUS [12]

SLAVES	FREE BORN
Lynch	Miller
Smalls	Walls
DeLarge	Ransier
Murray	Elliott
Haralson	Cain
Turner	Revels
Nash	Rapier
Long	O'Hara
Bruce	Langston
Hyman	
White	
Cheatham	
Rainey	

[11] *Cong. Directory, passim.*

[12] *Ibid.*, supplemented by the contemporaneous press and information received in recent letters.

With these facts in mind it is now pertinent to examine the work of the Negro in the Senate and in the House; to survey the many bitter contests in which the Negro was the loser; and, finally, to attempt an evaluation of his participation in the national legislature.

II

THE NEGRO IN THE SENATE

BECAUSE THE AMERICAN people have maintained the very highest standards for membership in their Senate, it has often been called the greatest deliberative body in the world. The memory of Calhoun, Clay, Webster, and others has served to exalt the Senate in the public mind. Therefore, it was more startling for a Negro to be elected to it than to be elected to the House of Representatives. The Negroes and their white allies were greatly elated by this honor, and the Southern whites were correspondingly depressed and humiliated. Since the two Negro senators were both from Mississippi, a survey of politics within that state will serve to explain how such a complete reversal had taken place in this former Democratic slave state and how the election of Senator Revels was a natural thing in the new situation there.

The eyes of the nation had been on Mississippi since 1865. The "Andrew Johnson legislature" at that time enacted a so-called black code, which provoked much Northern criticism. It regulated vagrancy, with the right to hire a Negro out to pay his fine, and it forbade intermarriage of the races.[1] The Chicago *Tribune* indulged in its favorite pastime of denouncing the South and threatened that the men of the North would convert the state into a frog pond before they would allow any such laws.[2] By 1867, under the congressional plan,

[1] James W. Garner, *Reconstruction in Mississippi*, pp. 113 ff.
[2] *Ibid.*, p. 115, n. 3.

this action was in process. By the new registration of voters 60,167 Negroes were put on the lists and only 46,636 whites. The Negro voters were in a majority in thirty-three out of sixty-one counties. This meant Negro members in the legislature and also strength in senatorial elections. The following counties had large black majorities: Adams, Bolivar, Claiborne, Hinds, Issaquena, Lowndes, Noxubee, Warren, Washington, Yazoo, and Tunica. Adams was the home of Revels and Lynch; Bolivar was the home of Bruce.[8]

The first Republican convention ever held in the state met at Jackson, September 10, 1867, and about a third of its members were ex-slaves. The Reverend James Lynch was one of the Negro members and resented the use of the word "colored" in the roll of delegates. He moved that the color of each delegate's hair be noted instead.[4] This supersensitiveness is characteristic and will come out often in our story. In the constitutional convention which met in 1868 there were seventeen Negroes, the majority of them without education or political experience. But in the Republican state convention of that year the Negroes, although present, were slighted in the matter of nominations. This caused loud protests, and Fitzhugh, a member of the constitutional convention, announced his withdrawal from the party.[5]

Consequently, in 1869 the Negroes had to be given more recognition, and James Lynch was nominated for Secretary of State and was elected with the rest of the Republican ticket. Lynch was an unusual Negro, with a good education and an eloquent tongue, who had come down from Indiana. He was a Methodist preacher of fine ability and was in great demand as an orator during the campaign. The Democrats were not

[8] *Ibid.*, pp. 113-115.
[4] *Ibid.*, p. 180 and p. 181, n. 1. James Lynch is not to be confused with John R. Lynch.
[5] *Ibid.*, pp. 187 f.

anxious to meet him in joint debate. No doubt he would have gone to Congress later, but he died suddenly in 1872.[6]

In this same campaign H. R. Revels was nominated from Adams County as a compromise candidate for state senate. He was practically unknown, but was believed to be able and above the average in intelligence. He was an African Methodist Episcopal pastor in Natchez; he had never voted, or made a political speech, or even attended a political meeting before. On his nomination he spoke briefly, making a favorable impression, and thus launched his spectacular political career. At the time, the Republican nomination was equivalent to election, and his majority was over 1,500.[7]

When the state legislature convened in January, 1870, Revels opened the Senate with prayer; and it helped make him a United States senator. On a joint ballot the Negroes cast about a fourth of the votes and demanded one of the three vacancies which were to be filled. The whites were willing for Revels to have the short, unexpired term, as it was understood Ames would get the five year term and Alcorn the full term succeeding the unexpired term. James Lynch was first suggested as the Negro representative; but he had just been elected to state office, and it was considered unwise to create a vacancy which would cause a new election. Revels was next considered, his impressive prayer having made him the logical man; but there were white candidates still in the way. A special to the Memphis *Avalanche*, sent during the balloting, mentioned Flournoy and Eggleston, but not Revels. However, Eggleston's name was withdrawn, and Revels was elected January 20, 1870. It was felt that he was the strongest member of his race to balance Ames and Alcorn, whites, already chosen. He was first nominated in a Negro conference, then in party caucus, and was elected in joint session. Only

---

[6] *Ibid.*, pp. 243, 246; John R. Lynch, *Facts of Reconstruction*, p. 31.
[7] *Ibid.*, pp. 40-44.

one Republican voted against him, offering constitutional grounds, not personal ones.[8]

Revels had become famous practically over night, and everyone was eager to know something concerning him. Hiram Rhoades Revels was born September 27, 1822, at Fayetteville, North Carolina. He was a free Negro, a fact which took the edge from the joy of the Radicals, who would have exulted more in the elevation of an ex-slave. At an uncertain date he moved to Indiana and attended the Quaker Seminary in Union County. Next he moved to Darke County, Ohio, and attended a seminary there. During the period of his education he was ordained in the African Methodist Episcopal ministry, 1845, at Baltimore, Maryland. Then he seems to have returned to Illinois, for he graduated from Knox College at Bloomington. He lectured among his people in Indiana, Illinois, Missouri, Kansas, Kentucky, and Tennessee, and taught school in St. Louis, Missouri. Also he preached in Cincinnati, St. Louis, Pittsburgh, and Baltimore.[9]

He was in Baltimore when the Civil War began and assisted in organizing the first two Negro regiments in Maryland. Then in 1863 he moved to St. Louis, founded a large school for freedmen, and helped recruit a Negro regiment there. In 1864 he joined the federal army in Mississippi as chaplain of a Negro regiment. He also helped in the work of the Freedmen's Bureau and in extending protection to Negro troops. When crossing from Vicksburg to Jackson to establish schools and churches, he came near being captured by bushwhackers, but he was warned and escaped. He returned to the

---

[8] Memphis *Daily Avalanche*, January 16, 1870; Lynch, *op. cit.*, pp. 40-44; *Cong. Directory*, p. 1454.

[9] Lynch, *op. cit.*, pp. 44-47; Memphis *Daily Avalanche*, January 16 and 21, 1870; William H. Barnes, *History of Congress. The Forty-first Congress of the United States*, p. 108. (Hereinafter cited *History of Forty-first Congress*.)

The *Cong. Directory* gives 1827 as the year of Revels' birth, but the context shows that date to be erroneous. All other sources agree on the year 1822.

North in 1864 and preached at Louisville and Leavenworth, Kansas. In 1866, he settled in Natchez, Mississippi, and combined preaching with participation in politics, being elected as alderman 1868, and to the state senate in 1870. In fairness it must be said that he entered politics reluctantly, because he feared his elevation would lead to racial friction; however, he yielded to the urging of his friends. He had plenty of precedents for his actions, for practically every other Negro preacher was deep in politics. Many of them prostituted the pulpit to partisan purposes—something which, it seems, Revels never did.[10]

However, it is no discredit to Revels to say that he would have died unknown except for his election to the Senate. The reports from the Savannah *News* will indicate his obscurity. In the first report he was called "Kevalls," this was changed to "Ravel" two days later, and it was only after a week that his name appeared correctly. This usually partisan Democratic paper accepted the situation philosophically and said his election met with general Democratic approval. The hope was expressed that Revels would secure a seat next to Sumner and be as black as the ace of spades.[11] On the other hand, the Memphis *Avalanche* in an editorial blamed the Southerners for political folly and blindness in not accepting Negro suffrage as settled, and stated that the resulting agitation had driven the Negroes into an alliance with the Radicals. The people of Mississippi could have averted the election of Revels, had they looked facts squarely in the face before, instead of taking counsel of passion and prejudice.[12] This sounds plausible enough; but Memphis, Tennessee, is not in the Black Belt, while Jackson, Mississippi, is, and such circumstances usually controlled the attitude of the masses and

---

10 Barnes, *History of Forty-first Congress*, pp. 108-109.
11 Savannah *News*, January 21, 22, 27, 1870.
12 Memphis *Daily Avalanche*, January 22, 1870.

of the press. Also, the policy of conciliation was tried in several states, as we shall see, and was usually given up for a "straight-out" policy. However, the *Avalanche* made the best of the situation and remarked:

Seven cities contended for the honor of Homer's birth. How many will struggle for Revels' is yet a question. A week ago 5000 people had never heard his name or if heard, it was only to be forgotten. Now it will be the subject of 500 "leaders" and when Revels reaches Washington the reporters of all the great journals will interview him. Happy Revels. He is of popular manners and speaks with great ease, fluency, and generally in good taste. In his intercourse with all classes he conducts himself with decorousness that has won for him the regard of all his neighbors at home and of the members of the Mississippi Senate of which he is now a member.

Revels had lived in Memphis previously and had offered a very impressive prayer at the execution of a Negro murderer.[13]

But soon doubts arose as to Revels' eligibility. The New York *Herald* thought he would be excluded, as Menard had been, while the Chicago *Times* declared that he could not be a citizen before the year 1866, and that, therefore, he would not be eligible until nine years had elapsed—that is, in 1875. The Baltimore *Gazette* went even further in publishing charges that he was guilty of immoral conduct while a Kansas pastor, asserted that he had misappropriated church funds and in a drunken brawl had had whiskey bottles broken over his head.[14] These were only idle rumors; none was true. The Mobile *Register* appropriately remarked that if immorality were made a test the Senate would be swept clean of its members.[15] *The Nation* solved the question of eligibility very easily: The Dred Scott decision did not include free blacks because they

---

[13] *Ibid.*

[14] Mobile *Register* cites these January 27, February 1, 18, 1870.

[15] *Ibid.*, February 15, 1870.

had been recognized as citizens in earlier days. Anyway, the annexation of foreign territory had conferred citizenship at once, as in the case of Texas. *The Nation,* following Stevens' conquered province theory, regarded Mississippi as annexed foreign territory and claimed that Revels, when his state was readmitted, would at once fall heir to all rights of citizenship.[16]

The sable statesman left the editors to worry over these things while he speedily went to Washington to familiarize himself with society before taking up his official duties. He reached there January 30 and made his home on Capitol Hill with George T. Downing, a Negro who ran the Capitol Restaurant. There the Negro leaders came to call on him, and he announced his policy. Revels said that his large experience would help him in representing them and that he would use his own judgment on political questions. He had no peculiar measures to advocate and was opposed to extreme measures, which had hurt the party in Mississippi. He felt that both friends and foes were watching him; therefore, he felt a responsibility, one which deeply impressed him. We are also given an accurate account of his personal qualities at this time. He was tall, portly, of a benevolent expression and pleasant, impressive voice. He spoke with distinctness, as if thoroughly convinced of the views which he entertained.[17] During the interval of three weeks Revels was entertained by a Negro, Dr. Charles Purvis. Here he met the Negro elite of the capital on the first day he was in the city. Then he was honored at a dinner where the races mingled. His colleague, Ames, was there with other senators, and the whole Mississippi delegation in the House. The party lingered long and much comment was aroused. To cap the climax, John W. Forney entertained Revels and had President Grant and cabi-

---

[16] *The Nation,* February 3, 1870.

[17] *National Republican,* January 31, 1870; Memphis *Daily Avalanche* quoting Louisville *Courier Journal,* February 2, 1870.

net members present. Grant received him with great kindness and hoped he would be admitted without difficulty.[18]

The stage was set for a very dramatic chapter when Wilson on February 23 presented Revels' credentials. The charge was sometimes made that even the Radicals did not really want a Negro in Congress, that they were using the issue for politics in order to get the Negro vote and to keep the Negro loyal to the party. It was further alleged that the Radicals would be glad to see Revels rejected. However, the facts apparently do not support this statement, as the Radicals were only too glad to have this opportunity to humiliate the South.[19] The fact that Revels' credentials had been signed by General Ames caused the question to be debated as to the ability of an army officer to certify to civil elections. Davis denied the eligibility of Revels under the nine year clause, and Stockton insisted that the credentials be referred to a committee. Nye rejoiced that a Negro was replacing Jefferson Davis. The debate was so prolonged that no vote was taken that day.[20]

On February 24 the debate was resumed, and the day passed without a decision. Howard thought it remarkable, indeed, for Revels to replace Davis. Cameron made it even more dramatic by relating an incident of 1861. Just before Davis left Washington Cameron had said, "I believe, in the justice of God, that a Negro some day will come and occupy your seat." Cameron now rejoiced that the prophecy had come true.[21]

On the third day of the contest Wilson made the principal argument in favor of Revels. He, also, rejoiced that a black

[18] *National Republican*, January 31, 1870; Claude G. Bowers, *The Tragic Era*, pp. 294 f.

[19] Mobile *Register*, February 16, 27, 1870.

[20] Savannah *News*, February 1, 1870; *Congressional Globe*, 41st Cong., 2nd Sess., pp. 1503 f.

[21] *Ibid.*

man had come up from Mississippi. This justified Stockton's rejoinder that Revels was being admitted because he was a Negro, not because he was a legal representative, for a white applicant would have been subjected to committee investigation. Sumner spoke very briefly in support of Revels. Late in the day the vote was taken on referring the matter of his admission to a committee and, also, on the direct question of admission. In both, the vote was 48 to 8 in favor of Revels; thereupon he was escorted to the desk by Wilson, sworn in, and seated at 4:40 P.M. on February 25. The New York *Times* gave a vivid description of the scene. The galleries were packed, and even the aisles were crowded. When Colfax asked Revels to come forward, the proverbial pin could have been heard to drop. The vast crowd then stood, but made no demonstration. Revels seemed self-possessed and dignified.[22]

He lost little time in plunging into the routine of the Senate and made his maiden speech within three weeks. He was put on an insignificant committee, the one on Education and Labor. Although not a chairman, he made several reports to the Senate from the committee. Only three minor bills were introduced by him, and none of them was passed. On the other hand, he presented eighteen petitions, many of them commendable in that they asked for removal of political disabilities of individuals; one from his state legislature asked for this removal for all its citizens. In addition to his official duties he found that the whole Negro race of 5,000,000 depended on him to give them advice and offices. Finally, he was so pressed by them that he gave orders to the doorkeeper to bring him no cards during the session.[23]

These activities were merely initiating him into senatorial procedure and clearing the stage for his first formal speech. The Radicals, wanting more publicity for their protégé, ar-

[22] *Ibid.*, pp. 1542-1544; New York *Times*, February 26, 1870.
[23] *Cong. Globe*, 41st Cong., 2nd Sess., pp. 1561-1568.

ranged to have him speak long before a new white senator is accustomed to do so. On Sunday, March 13, the Negro churches announced that Revels would speak on Monday. Although Negroes thronged into the galleries on that day and crowded out the whites, their dusky hero did not perform then but was given a place on the calendar for Wednesday. Again the galleries were packed with both sexes of both races. Many persons from the House had come across to hear him. The best "pens" in the nation were there to broadcast this gala event, and even the Southern press gave him due credit for making a good impression.[24]

The Radicals had wished to seat him in Davis' old chair because of the spectacular effect, but Ross of Kansas had it and refused to give it up. Instead of number thirty-five Revels had to take number nineteen, on the opposite side and at the extreme end of the row. But for this occasion he came over to the center of the hall and stood at Fenton's desk.[25]

Although he was not to speak until 1:00 P.M., by 9:00 A.M. ladies were in their gallery, just as in the days of Toombs, Wigfall, and Davis. "Never since the birth of the republic has such an audience been assembled under one single roof. It embraced the greatest and the least American citizens." So thought the writer for the Philadelphia *Press*. He had heard Jefferson Davis speak and by comparison considered Revels' manner much preferable.[26] He was congratulated at the finish by Cameron, Drake, Fenton, Stewart, Sumner, and many others.[27]

Going to the official record we find the speech good, con-

---

[24] New York *Times*, March 7, 1870; Memphis *Avalanche*, March 19, 1870; *Cong. Globe*, 41st Cong., 2nd Sess., pp. 1986-1989.

[25] New York *Times*, March 15, 17, 1870; Philadelphia *Inquirer*, March 17, 1870.

[26] *The Nation*, March 10, 1870; diagram of the seating for this session, *Cong. Globe*, 41st Cong., 2nd Sess., p. v; Philadelphia *Inquirer*, March 17, 1870; Memphis *Daily Avalanche*, March 19, 1870.

[27] Barnes, *History of Forty-first Congress*, pp. 109-111.

sidering everything, but not notable enough to call for extravagant expressions. The question was the readmission of Georgia, and Revels felt that he had a personal interest; he claimed that the freedmen there were being oppressed and that the federal government should protect them by defeating the pending Bingham Amendment. Revels showed that the Negroes were peaceable during and after the war. His conclusion was effective, "And now, sir, I protest in the name of truth and human rights against any and every attempt to fetter the hands of 100,000 white and colored citizens of the State of Georgia." Morton obtained the floor and declared that the Senate, in getting Revels in Davis' place, had lost nothing in intelligence while it had gained much in patriotism and loyalty.[28] Although it was the popular thing for congressmen to abuse Jefferson Davis, it is pleasant to note that Revels did not join this practice.

Revels showed his tolerance in his next speech, delivered on May 17. The removal of political disabilities was under discussion when Revels expressed himself in favor of leniency for all rather than for individuals. He asserted that the only test should be loyalty, that in Mississippi harmony prevailed, and that all were in favor of amnesty. If all were forgiven and none disfranchised in Mississippi, Revels might have less chance in politics than Davis, but that did not change his attitude.[29]

As soon as the news of his first success on the floor reached the Mississippi Senate, Morgan moved to create a new county to be named Revels; but this was only a gesture and received no serious support.[30] However, he was honored out in the world in a more substantial, if less sensational, way. He was much in demand for public lectures even though the directors

---

[28] *Cong. Globe*, 41st Cong., 2nd Sess., pp. 1986-1989.
[29] *Ibid.*, p. 3520.
[30] Memphis *Daily Avalanche*, March 19, 1870.

of the Philadelphia Academy of Music had refused to let him appear there in a very popular and highly respectable course of lectures; the lone Democrat on the board had voted to admit him as any other lecturer, and *The Nation* believed that public opinion was decidedly against the directors. Yet their decision stood in this, the state of Thaddeus Stevens, the arch apostle of race equality. This occurred April 1, but in July Revels was welcomed to Cincinnati to deliver his lecture, "The Tendency of our Age." [31]

During this summer Revels gained notice by appointing a Negro to West Point. The cadet failed to pass and soon dropped out. *The Nation* pronounced it "a very foolish and cruel thing as far as the boy and his family are concerned and a very injudicious thing as far as the colored race is concerned." [32]

At the beginning of the next session he was put on the District of Columbia Committee and so became especially interested in the freedmen there, but he took even more interest in the levees and early introduced a bill to repair and construct levees in Mississippi.[33] On January 11, 1871, he spoke on this subject in a very able and appropriate way. Indeed, after a careful reading of all his speeches this one seems to be the best, since it was nonpartisan and a typical southern, cotton-country speech, such as would be made today by Byrnes or Smith of South Carolina. He surveyed the cotton culture of the world, showing that although India was America's most dangerous rival the South was unequaled by any country of the globe in soil and climate. His bill failed to pass, however, as did all others that he introduced.[34] One of these was of a nature to delight the heart of an Octavus Cohen

[31] *The Nation*, April 7, 1870; The New York *Times*, July 11, 1870.
[32] Bowers, *op. cit.*, p. 296—quoting *The Nation*, June 9, 1870.
[33] *Cong. Globe*, 41st Cong., 3rd Sess., pp. 40, 116.
[34] *Ibid.*, pp. 425, 426. The Jackson *Pilot*, January 18, 1870, gave front page space to this speech.

or an Irvin Cobb. It proposed to incorporate the Grand Tabernacle of Galilean Fishermen, but even this impressive name was not sufficient to carry the bill through.[35]

Since this was the short session, little was done by the Senate, and, naturally, Revels' part was insignificant. February 8, 1871, he delivered his swan song—a speech concerning mixed schools in the District of Columbia. Revels favored the proposal because he thought it would break down prejudice and at the same time not lead to social equality. The same, in his opinion, would apply to railroads and other common carriers. He was careful to say: "The white race has no better friend than I. I am true to my own race ... but at the same time, I would not have anything done which would harm the white race." If the Republican party really discriminated against the white race by legislation, he would leave the party, he alleged. In closing he reminded the Senate: "What I have said I have said in kindness; and I hope it will be received in that spirit." Partisans who were so fond of comparing him to Jefferson Davis lost a good chance here, for Revels' conciliatory note sounded considerably like Davis' farewell with its plea for good will.[36]

Governor Alcorn at first declined to take the place vacated by Revels, and there was a good prospect that Revels would be elected for a full term. But by March 25 Alcorn had told the legislature that he would serve and would be present at the opening of the next session. It was reported that Revels would be agent in the South for the Congressional Temperance Society. Just before the end of his term Revels gave an interview summing up his year in Washington. He deplored the sad but common fact in politics that even his party press and his own race sometimes distorted facts. On this occasion he spoke with more brilliance than was usually at-

[35] *Cong. Globe,* 41st Cong., 3rd Sess., p. 664.
[36] *Ibid.,* pp. 1059-1060.

tributed to him. He had broken with Sumner on Santo Domingo, but, as Sumner had lost caste, the defection did not hurt Revels.[37]

Soon after his retirement he gave another interview in which he admitted that he had received fair treatment, even in the matter of patronage. Boutwell, Secretary of Treasury, had been especially kind. Revels had been much besieged by office seekers, but he had usually dodged them unless they had proved their friendship earlier. From now on he expected to represent the race even more comprehensively than he had in the Senate.[38]

If his votes during these two sessions are examined, Revels appears as more of a partisan than his speeches would indicate, in spite of the fact that he was absent when many important votes were taken. In the second session he voted for the eligibility of Ames, for the carpetbag government of Texas and for the readmission of Texas under this regime, for enforcement of the Fifteenth Amendment, for the change in naturalization by striking out the word "white." All these were partisan measures, and Revels was partisan on them; yet he also voted to abolish the franking privilege, a nonpartisan measure.[39] In the next session his record is much the same. He favored a federal election law with penalties, opposed making public the proceedings of the committee on Southern outrages, and supported federal aid for steamship service to Mexico.[40] This was a time of partisanship, and he should not be censured unduly on this score. Revels was to prove later that he could rise above party if necessary.

Alcorn College had just been established for Negroes of Mississippi, and Alcorn himself now appointed Revels as first president of it. This institution received good support

[37] *National Republican*, February 23, March 7, 8, 14, 25, 1871.
[38] Jackson *Pilot*, March 16, 1871.
[39] *Cong. Globe*, 41st Cong., 2nd Sess., pp. 2349-2372, 3015, 3521, 4003, 5123.
[40] *Ibid.*, 3rd Sess., pp. 1208, 1640, 1817.

from the state, and it flourished for several years. The University at Oxford was open to Negroes, but none ever tried to enter, probably because of the liberal appropriation for them at Alcorn and at several normal schools. In 1874 Governor Ames dismissed Revels, and sixty students left with him as a protest. His successor proved so unsuitable in general that in March, 1875, the legislature sent a committee to investigate. It was reported that the school was a den of lewdness, drunkenness, and iniquity. A Democratic paper remarked that Revels' connection with the school had been a redeeming feature. "His character as a man of piety, and integrity was unimpeached. But he was dismissed by Ames and since then pandemonium has reigned." [41] At that time Revels did not stand well enough with the Republican bosses to secure the appointment again, but when the Democrats regained the state he was put in charge in August, 1876. Again it was a Democratic paper that predicted a useful future for the school under his direction.[42]

He had acted as ad interim Secretary of State for a short time in 1873 and again was interested in politics in 1875. The Democrats were making a great fight then to regain the state and many Negroes left the Republicans and helped decisively defeat their former party. Revels was one of these and explained his stand in a long letter to President Grant. This letter was published widely and caused much comment. In it he charged that the Republicans had forfeited their right to remain in power by following a corrupt and dishonest course and that all good men had combined to defeat them. Ames is not named but is clearly indicated in the general condemnation.[43]

Before resuming work at Alcorn he was in New Orleans,

[41] Natchez *Daily News and Courier*, March 5, 1875; Garner, *op. cit.*, pp. 369, 370.

[42] New Orleans *Times*, August 6, 1876.

[43] Garner, *op. cit.*, pp. 399-400; *Cong. Directory*, p. 1454.

June, 1876, having been designated by the General Conference to edit the *Southwestern Advocate*. He preached there
and made a very good impression. But the plans for the
paper did not work out at that time, and he left the city. After
his second term as college head he returned to religious work
and made his home at Holly Springs, Mississippi. He became
district superintendent in his church, and it was while attend-
ing a church conference at Aberdeen, Mississippi, that he died,
January 16, 1901.[44]

Thus ended the career of the first Negro in national politics. He blazed the way, and it was easier for the others to
follow. Revels was not as intelligent as Elliott, nor as shrewd
as Smalls, but no later Negro in politics was received any
better by the whites of both parties and sections. At the same
time he had not neglected the interests of his own people.

The next Negro to serve in the Senate had a distinction
all his own. Blanche K. Bruce was the only Negro in American history to serve a regular term in the United States Senate. He was quite different from Revels, but his career in
some respects was just as remarkable. He was born a slave in
Prince Edward County, Virginia, March 1, 1841. He was a
quadroon or octoroon and was light yellow. His mother had
been the slave of a wealthy planter, and young Bruce was a
pet and often said he saw none of the horrors of slavery. Instead, he did as he liked and was educated by a tutor. At any
time he could have escaped but had no reason for doing so.
Yet he was nominally a slave and so was carried to Missouri
several years before the Civil War. At Brunswick he learned
the printer's trade.[45]

About this time Bruce was also in St. Louis. One day a
gentleman in a hurry to reach his steamer pressed a Negro

---

[44] *Ibid.;* New Orleans *Republican,* June 8, 27, 28, 1876.
[45] New York *Times,* March 18, 1898; John W. Cromwell, *The Negro in American History,* p. 164.

boy into service to carry his very heavy valise, threatening him with dire penalties if he did not get there on time. Having reached the boat, the gentleman failed to pay the boy anything. Years passed and the traveler became a Senator, Senator Bogy from Missouri. On one occasion Bogy, sponsoring a local bill, solicited Bruce's support. This was promised, but at the same time Bruce disclosed that he was the contemptible little Negro whom Bogy still owed for his service. The amount compounded was quickly offered and refused. Then the two men became good friends and so continued until Bogy's death. Such a startling upset could have happened only in the United States at this time, and the story seems to be authenticated.[46]

In 1861 Bruce's young master, who was about his age, enlisted in the Confederate army, and Bruce escaped to Hannibal, Missouri. There he organized the first school in the country exclusively for Negroes. After the war he took a special two year course at Oberlin College. Then he went to Mississippi at just the opportune time, since there was a good chance there for intelligent and capable men. He reached Jackson with little money—exactly seventy-five cents—and no friends, but both defects were soon remedied. His pleasing personality won the good will of the state authorities. Starting in 1869 as sergeant-at-arms of the state senate he held a succession of local offices, being at different times county assessor, tax collector, sheriff, superintendent of schools, and member of the levee board. He also found time to engage in planting on a large scale and became wealthy. At one time he had to give bond aggregating $120,000 and did this with the aid of his white neighbors, who had confidence in his honesty.[47]

These honors made Bruce much more logical a candidate

---

[46] Norman B. Wood, *The White Side of a Black Subject*, pp. 405-406.

[47] New York *Times*, March 18, 1898; Lynch, *op. cit.*, p. 80; G. W. Williams, *History of the Negro Race in America*, II, 445.

than Revels had been. Indeed he came near to being honored too much by being made lieutenant-governor, but he refused to accept that nomination believing it would side-track him from the higher one. Revels' election practically came unsought, but Bruce went out and worked for his. Consequently, by the time the party caucus of the legislature met Bruce had the backing of Ames, and on the second ballot received 52 votes out of 88. This was January 31, and on February 3, 1874, he was elected against very weak opposition, securing even the votes of three Democratic senators.[48]

Naturally during the year of waiting he could not be active in politics, but a Democratic paper kindly gave him some unusual advice. Bruce was a bachelor and was advised for his political benefit to remain one. Pinchback had been rejected by the Senate because the senatorial wives would not associate with Mrs. Pinchback, although their husbands had passed the Civil Rights Bill by a large majority. At any rate, Bruce did wait three years to marry.[49]

Bruce was present March 5, 1875, when the special session met and he received more attention than anyone except Andrew Johnson, who had just returned to the Senate. Bruce was said to be a man of fine physique, good countenance, and gentlemanly bearing. In general appearance he strikingly resembled King Kalakaua, of Hawaii. On account of a grudge against Ames, Alcorn did not escort his colleague to the desk to be sworn in. Bruce was embarrassed but was starting up alone when Senator Conkling noticed it and accompanied him. For this Bruce was duly grateful and several years later named his only son Roscoe Conkling.[50]

In this short session, which lasted until March 24, Bruce took no part in the discussion on the Louisiana situation. He

[48] Lynch, op. cit., p. 77; Vicksburg Times, February 1, 4, 1874; Mobile Register, February 5, 1874.

[49] Natchez Daily News and Courier, August 19, 1874.

[50] New York Times, March 6, 1875; Lynch, op. cit., pp. 78-79.

always voted with his party but had nothing to say, although thirty-three other members spoke at length. In this way he acquired the title of "silent senator," but he was able to overcome this reputation later and to become an able speaker. His committee assignments, Manufactures, Pensions, Education and Labor, were as good as the usual.[51]

He was present December 6 when the regular session met, but there were rumors that he, Dorsey, and Spencer were to be expelled for bribery in their elections. It was noted that only four members had bouquets, sent by admirers, on their desks, and that Bruce was one so remembered. His colleague, Alcorn, was absent over a month, but Bruce did not seize the chance to speak up for his state. In this, his first regular session, he introduced only one bill and that a racial one which was reported adversely. He presented two petitions, one of them asking for national prohibition by constitutional amendment. If original, this would have entitled him to considerable distinction, but it was not original.[52]

Although he was usually silent on the floor, he did much unofficial talking about the exclusion of Pinchback. Bruce declared that if Pinchback was not admitted the Negroes should make the best political terms they could with their old masters and let the Republican party "go to the devil," that Grant did not care for the South, and that Bruce would oppose his renomination and re-election. He even denounced Grant and the party in an executive session of the Senate and alarmed the leaders, who brought strong pressure to bear on him to be more moderate. He refused to go to the White House in answer to a summons from Grant, but he did subside. No doubt Bruce was holding out for better patronage, for he was too much of a partisan to bolt; and in 1880 he was a member

[51] *Congressional Record*, 44th Cong., Spec. Sess. Senate, pp. 1, 8, 9, and *passim*.

[52] *Ibid.*, 1st Sess., pp. 165, 308; New Orleans *Times*, December 7, 1875.

of the Grant bloc in the National Convention and voted for him thirty times.[53]

After a calendar year had passed, he at last gained courage to make a speech, March 3, 1876, on a resolution to admit Pinchback from Louisiana. He upheld briefly the validity of the election, arguing that if otherwise the Louisiana legislature was illegal and should be disowned, too. Also, he urged Pinchback's admission on practical rather than on abstract grounds, for this solution would stop the agitation and give Louisiana full representation. He was on the regulars' side in the vote, but this was the losing side.[54] He spoke at another time in favor of a resolution to investigate the election of 1875 in Mississippi. He declared that he had not wished to speak again until he became more familiar with senatorial procedure, but that duty to his constituents and state forced him to speak. He pointed out that in Mississippi the Republicans had had a majority of 20,000 in 1873; they now had a minority of 30,000. Nothing but fraud and intimidation could account, in his mind, for such a large shift, since Negroes made up ninety-five per cent of the Republican party and nothing had occurred to make them change. Most of the trouble he blamed on the White Leagues. He traced the great advances of his race in economic, moral, and social ways and held that the federal government should safeguard these fruits. Because the bulk of the Negroes would remain in the South on the soil, he claimed they should be protected there. His vote for the investigation was on the winning side this time.[55]

A special session of the Senate to try Belknap lasted from April 5 to August 1, 1876. Bruce attended all meetings but never opened his mouth except to vote. He voted on all five

[53] *Ibid.*, February 11, 12, 13, 1876; Cromwell, *op. cit.*, p. 170.
[54] *Cong. Rec.*, 44th Cong., 1st Sess., pp. 1444-1445, 1558.
[55] *Ibid.*, pp. 2101, 2119.

articles "not guilty for want of jurisdiction." Again he was on the winning side, for although a majority voted "guilty," there was not the two-thirds majority necessary to convict.[56]

In the memorable campaign of 1876 he took an active part in Mississippi and Louisiana for Hayes and Wheeler. The Memphis *Appeal* claimed he advised the Negroes at his home at Bolivar to vote the Democratic ticket. Bruce denied this and explained that he had simply advised them against violence and had urged quiet performance of their duty as voters.[57] So his record as a regular within the party was preserved.

In the next session he again earned his title of the "silent senator," with a single exception; without even gaining the floor he interrogated Senator Key, who was speaking on alleged outrages in Louisiana. Key had doubted that such outrages had been committed by white men, and Bruce asked if he then accused the Negroes. Key explained he meant that only savages could have acted so; Bruce again assumed that his race was blamed, but Key insisted that Bruce was mistaken. This two-minute interjection was Senator Bruce's sole oratorical effort during the whole session. He did introduce one private bill and submit two petitions, none of which received any consideration. He introduced the petition for prohibition again and also one for improvement of the Mississippi River.[58]

The new Forty-fifth Congress had two special sessions before the regular one in December, one of the Senate alone, and the other of both Houses. Bruce attended faithfully, always being present on the opening day whether he had anything to say or not. He was appointed on the same regular committees, and in addition he was made chairman of a select committee on Mississippi River levees. This was indeed an honor, as there were so many other Mississippi Valley mem-

[56] *Ibid., Impeachment Trial W. W. Belknap*, pp. 118-120.
[57] *National Republican*, October 11, 1876.
[58] *Cong. Rec.*, 44th Cong., 2nd Sess., pp. 264, 679, 736, 1547.

bers who would have been especially suitable. Serving under him on the committee were Blaine, Conover, Cockrell, and Harris. No doubt this was an interesting experience for the two Southern Democrats, Cockrell and Harris.[59] It was at this time that L. Q. C. Lamar came up to enter the Senate from Mississippi. Because of the disturbances in the Mississippi elections for the legislature which elected L. Q. C. Lamar to the Senate, there was some question as to the validity of his election. Bruce took no part in this discussion, although it was a partisan move to keep Lamar out; on the vote Bruce put partisanship aside and voted to seat him. This was carried, and it is interesting to note the good will which prevailed throughout the rest of Lamar's life between these representatives of bitterly hostile groups back in Mississippi. There was no suspicion of a political agreement, but each must have respected in the other the real man beneath the partisan.[60] Bruce's only other activities in this session were to present a petition asking federal aid for emigrants to Liberia, and to get his position on the Manufactures Committee transposed. The chairman of this committee had resigned, leaving Bruce as the senior member and acting chairman; he asked that Rollins be made chairman, and this was done.[61]

Both Houses were called into special session October 15, and naturally very little business could be transacted in the short time before the regular session. Even then it is somewhat surprising to note Bruce's sole comment. He was asked if he were paired with the Senator from Florida and replied in an impersonal way, "He is not. He is paired with the Senator from Alabama." [62] At any rate Bruce voted regularly, usually with the Radicals. He voted against reducing the army, against admitting Butler from South Carolina, but for

[59] *Ibid.*, 45th Cong., Spec. Sess. Senate, p. 39.
[60] *Ibid.*, p. 15.
[61] *Ibid.*, pp. 364, 414.
[62] *Ibid.*, p. 700.

admitting Kellogg of Louisiana.[63] Now the case of Butler was exactly like the one from Mississippi, as it concerned election disorders, except that Butler personally was charged with more than Lamar; yet Bruce in this case felt he must vote with his party.

After two and a half years' experience Bruce seems to have become accustomed to the routine when the Forty-fifth Congress met in regular session December 3, 1877. Several pension bills of his were at last passed and signed by the President, though his other bills failed.[64] Several petitions were presented by him on prohibition and on refund of the cotton tax, but none of them received consideration. However, the last one gave Bruce a chance to put aside his bias, and advocate the refund of the cotton tax collected from Southern farmers.[65]

Bruce seems to have gained confidence by this time in his speaking ability. In the memorial exercise for Oliver P. Morton, he made his longest speech up to that time. Besides giving a general tribute to Morton, he lauded him especially as a friend of the Negro. He asserted that next to Lincoln and Sumner the Negroes knew Morton best and respected him as highly as any other.[66] Again he spoke well against having separate Negro regiments in the army. He thought there should be no distinction in the army, since there were already mixed crews in the navy. Even if such action should result in Negroes being turned down by recruiting officers, it would be better. The Negro should by now be able to stand on his own resources or go down. Thurman complained that Bruce talked so low that he could hear very little. Evidently his oratorical powers still needed development.[67]

[63] *Ibid.*, pp. 423, 712, 797.
[64] *Ibid.*, 2nd Sess., pp. 3454, 4791.
[65] *Ibid.*, pp. 116, 1360, 1929, 2598.
[66] *Ibid.*, pp. 382-383.
[67] *Ibid.*, pp. 2440-2441, 2442.

Outside of Congress, Bruce was especially interested at this time in the migration of the Negroes from the South. Many were going to Kansas, and there was dissension even among the Negro leaders as to the proper course. This cannot be discussed here, except to notice that Bruce favored emigration to Liberia on a large scale.[68]

During the recess of 1878 Bruce married Josephine Wilson of Cleveland. She was of a good family and even nearer white than Bruce. She was fond of social life, and they had an extensive bridal tour in Europe. Secretary of State Evarts gave their visit a semiofficial tinge by writing to United States diplomats in Europe to give them a good reception. As a result they were received with honors, both by American diplomats and by European statesmen. This was true especially in England and France, but also in Belgium, Holland, Germany, and Switzerland, for they found no racial discrimination anywhere. The *Times* went so far as to say that Bruce had a keen understanding of social proprieties and was as accomplished in his manner as any man in the Senate. They were away several months and on their return bought a home in Washington. This residence became a rendezvous for the circle of distinguished friends with which he and his wife were identified. She was tactful enough to avoid any racial and political quarrel, such as occurred in Washington a few years ago, and she seems to have been a real helpmate. Instead of being dependent on white society, they had created their own.[69] More stress has been given this because of the influence social success often had on the political fortunes of a man, and also

[68] Letter to Murat Halstead, February, 1878, in *Woodson Collection*, Library of Congress. Bruce wrote a good, clear hand and misspelled only one word.

[69] New York *Times*, December 7, 1878, March 18, 1898; Clement Richardson, *National Cyclopedia of the Colored Race*, p. 534; *National Republican*, December 30, 1878.

Wives of Supreme Court Justices and of members of both Houses visited Mrs. Bruce at her home.—William J. Simmons, *Men of Mark*, p. 702.

because we rarely have accounts of the wives and families of these black Congressmen.

Bruce was in place when the Senate convened December 2, and it was noticed that he was surrounded on the floor by a circle of friends, just as were the recognized leaders—Blaine, Edmunds, Thurman, Bayard, and Lamar. Bruce secured the passage of two pension bills but failed on others. He was still active in trying to get through measures for improvement of the Mississippi River and development of the channel and levee system. He reported such a bill from his special com- mittee, and the Senate passed it; however, the session ended before the House could concur.[70]

February 14, 1879, was a red-letter day in his political career. Vice-President Wheeler was absent, and for some time Bruce presided over the Senate, making rulings and appropriate remarks, until he gave way to Morrill. Then Bruce obtained the floor to speak on the proposed Chinese immigration re- striction. He was in a dilemma, for it was considered a patriotic duty to exclude these Orientals because of their utter dis- similarity to American stock. But how could a Negro support any discrimination based mainly on the racial and color line? Would not such support convict him of gross inconsistency? Bruce met the situation frankly, on the broad ground of no discrimination.

Mr. President, I desire to submit a single remark. Representing as I do a people who but a few years ago were considered essen- tially disqualified from enjoying the privileges and immunities of American citizenship, and who have since been so successfully in- troduced into the body politic, and having large confidence in the strength and assimilative power of our institutions, I shall vote against the pending bill.[71]

Hayes called the Forty-sixth Congress in special session

---

[70] *Cong. Rec.*, 45th Cong., 3rd Sess., pp. 2298, 1045, 1055, 1114, 2315.
[71] *Ibid.*, pp. 1306-1307, 1314.

March 18, 1879, even though it was Democratic in both branches. Bruce was retained on the same committees, but Lamar was made chairman of the Mississippi River Committee. Bruce then asked to be excused from that committee and the one on Pensions, giving no reason. His request was granted; but a month later Lamar asked that the vacancy be filled, and Bruce was again appointed.[72] In the meantime he had received a special honor in being appointed chairman of a select committee on the Freedmen's Bank. He was assisted by Cameron and three Southern Democrats, Gordon, Withers, and Garland. Sometime later Bruce asked that his committee be given authority to go into all affairs connected with the Bank, to investigate the causes for its failure, and to make a speedy adjustment of its finances. All this was granted, together with power to sit during recess, to summon witnesses, and to take testimony.[73] On the other hand, he was not successful with the bills he introduced or the petitions he presented.[74]

At this session Bruce was paired with Lamar on all political questions, and this served to show up in a pleasing way their mutual courtesy. A bill passed the Senate to establish a Mississippi River Commission to consider improvements from head to mouth of the stream. Bruce was detained at home during the vote by sickness, but on his return Lamar asked permission for Bruce to record his vote. This was contrary to rules and could not be allowed, but the colleagues had a chance to reveal their sentiments. Bruce said he had come solely to vote for the bill, and Lamar remarked that Bruce had accomplished his purpose at any rate. Naturally, they voted on different sides in regard to the use of marshals and deputies instead of troops at the polls; Lamar was absent when the vote was recorded, and Bruce voted, forgetting his pair. He

[72] *Ibid.*, 46th Cong., 1st Sess., pp. 1, 15, 913.
[73] *Ibid.*, pp. 2863, 1392-1393.
[74] *Ibid.*, p. 1623.

soon discovered his mistake and asked to withdraw his own
vote, which request was granted.[75]

By September, 1879, Bruce realized that his party in Mississippi was doomed and that he had no chance whatever to be
re-elected. In fact, he had only served a few months before
his party was repudiated decisively. He planned to give up
his Mississippi residence at the end of his term, but the
Clarion did not think that he had one to give up or that he
had even been in the state since his election. However, he had
been in the state a few times. In November the Democrats
elected three-fourths of the state legislature, settling his fate
definitely. When it met in January, 1880, George was elected
to succeed Bruce, the latter receiving only four complimentary
votes. To console him for such an overwhelming defeat some
Mississippians resident in Washington presented him, through
Judge Tarbell, with a gold mounted cane as an expression of
good will and an endorsement of his public record. He responded in a modest, thoughtful reply.[76]

When Congress met in December 1879, Bruce knew that
he had lost in Congress; but might he not aspire to even
higher honors? Would not a Negro on the national ticket in
1880 help to keep the Negroes in line for Grant or some other
head of the ticket? This session seems to have been his very
best one. Of the twenty-one bills he introduced, the majority
were of a private nature; some, however, were worth while—
such bills as the one concerning the Geneva award for the
Alabama claims, the one for aid to education and railroad
construction, and the one for reimbursement of depositors in
the Freedmen's Bank.[77] Not one of these became a law, but
they show his wide range of interests.

[75] *Ibid.*, pp. 2226-2227, 2103, 2437.

[76] Jackson *Weekly Clarion*, September 3, November 19, 1879, January 28,
February 4, 1880.

[77] *Cong. Rec.*, 46th Cong., 2nd Sess., pp. 124, 338, 693, 836, 1619, 1920, 2053,
2303.

He spoke in behalf of admitting, free of duty, clothing sent from England to destitute Negroes in Kansas. He pointed out that Americans had sent, in a naval vessel, relief to the suffering Irish and so this measure would be in keeping. He would not discuss whether these Negroes should have left home or not; he was simply appealing in the names of hundreds who were starving. Also, he supported a more enlightened policy toward the Indians. He pointed out that our previous policy had been a selfish one and had left them at the mercy of adventurers, agents, and soldiers. The new proposal to divide lands among them would, he thought, make them permanent settlers; he did not think that this solution was visionary, but rather, that it could be worked out satisfactorily. Only two days later he was urging investigation of mistreatment of a Negro cadet at West Point and said, ironically, that probably a little time should be given to improvement of conditions there, as well as among the Indians. He had discouraged a Negro who wished Bruce to help him get in West Point.[78]

May 4, 1880, Bruce had the unusual experience of presiding over the Democratic Senate for some time. Vest had the floor at the time and bitterly assailed Kellogg and the Republican party in general.[79]

In Bruce's last session he continued on his same committees but did little else. Only a few bills were introduced by him, and none passed. One, proposing to buy the Freedman's Bank property, did pass the Senate but got no further. As his only success he was granted the discarded Senate furniture for the use of the Home for Colored Women and Children.[80]

Thus closed the official career of the first Negro to serve a full term in the Senate. Occasionally a Negro may be elected to the House, but it is highly improbable, under the present

[78] *Ibid.*, pp. 1042, 2195, 2196, 2249.
[79] *Ibid.*, pp. 2971-2972.
[80] *Ibid.*, pp. 146, 477, 668, 836.

method of election, that a majority of the voters in a state will ever send one to the Senate. What, then, was the verdict on this one? Probably the *Clarion's* estimate was as accurate as any. It said that Bruce had made as fair and impartial a representative of his people and party as could be found in the South. "If he has done no good, he has done no harm. One thing we can say about Bruce, he was always there to answer the roll call." [81]

He had always been active in national politics and was a member of the 1880 Republican Convention. As early as May he had been mentioned for the vice-presidency on the Grant ticket. Late in May it was said he was a thorn in the flesh of the Republicans. In June, just before the convention met, it was reported that Fred Douglass was pushing him for the nomination and that the Negroes as a race expected the honor, but it was a vain hope. Bruce was called to the chair to preside temporarily, but this was only a perfunctory gesture, and he received little applause. Yet it meant a great deal to Bruce later on, for at a critical stage when several delegates wanted the floor at once Bruce recognized Garfield; Garfield made such a good impression that he was nominated and when elected showed his gratitude to Bruce. [82]

Rumor next suggested him for a place in the cabinet. Chalmers of Mississippi was quoted as approving him and as saying that he would be agreeable to the South. The Pittsburgh *Post* said that Conkling would urge him for the cabinet, but that Bruce's wife would be the hindrance. [83] This was only talk, but he really was offered the position of Minister to Brazil or the third assistantship to the postmaster-general. These he refused and was then appointed register of the treasury. He was confirmed without reference to a committee

[81] Jackson *Weekly Clarion*, February 4, 1880.

[82] *Ibid.*, May 12, 26, June 2, 16, 1880; New York *Times*, March 18, 1898. Bruce did receive 8 votes for Vice-President—New York *Sun*, June 9, 1880.

[83] New York *Times*, quoting Pittsburgh *Post*, January 20, 1881.

fter a complimentary speech by his former colleague, Lamar.[84] Taking office in May, 1881, he held it through the Garfield-Arthur term, retiring in 1885. He filled the place quietly, as there was no chance for display, but Negro historians saw the spectacular in it, anyway. Simmons said it was very dramatic that Bruce's signature was necessary to make worthless paper into money and added that the same black hand which wrote his name would have been cut off before the war for writing it.[85] Williams declared, "From a penniless slave he has risen to the position of writing his name on the currency of the country." [86] These statements stretch the truth to make a point, for Bruce never had been a downtrodden, penniless slave, and as a slave his "black hand" had often written his name.

During this time he was able to render his race a service, unofficially. From November, 1884, to May, 1885, the World's Cotton Exposition was held in New Orleans, and he had charge of the Negro exhibit. This was the first public display of Negro achievement in arts, inventions, and handicraft, and Bruce managed it so well that he received much favorable comment from the press. A white Southerner recalls, after many years, the creditable work of Bruce at that time, saying that he was indefatigable and took becoming pride in seeing his people get their just dues, and that the work they had done for freedom would show up well. Wilson says Bruce was "most courteous in manner, punctual in duties, a fine statesman of his race." [87]

Although not active in politics at this time, nevertheless he was accused by the Washington *Post* of having no higher regard for his race than to scheme how best to utilize its votes for the benefit of Republican office holders. Yet after Cleve-

[84] Richardson, *op. cit.*, p. 534; Williams, *op. cit.*, II, 446.
[85] *Op. cit.*, pp. 702-703.
[86] *Op. cit.*, II, 446.
[87] Peter M. Wilson, *Southern Exposure*, p. 150; Cromwell, *op. cit.*, p. 170.

land's election, when the Negroes were disturbed by malicious stories of re-enslavement, Bruce was appealed to as a representative Negro to reassure the race. Bruce complied and declared, "The greatest harmony has existed between the white and colored population, and Mr. Blaine's charges of intimidation and violence at the polls are entirely false."

In 1885 he was back in private life and devoted much time to lecturing. He made speeches far and wide, for he had developed a facility and power of expression that made him one of the most fluent men of the race. His services were in demand next to Langston's and Douglass' for anniversaries and other special occasions. He was always ready to respond for the good of his race. We are told that he was of splendid physique, above the average in height, broad shouldered, and erect. His expression and manner were friendly and yet firm. His photographs, as shown by Woodson and Lynch, reveal a man of impressive appearance.[89] By October, 1886, his reputation had won for him a series of one hundred speaking engagements at one hundred dollars a night.[90] Harrison appointed him recorder of deeds for the District of Columbia and he held the place until 1893, when he again retired for Democratic administration. At the same time he was made a trustee of the public schools of Washington and served for seven years. After McKinley's election in 1896, when there was speculation concerning the possibility of having a Negro in the cabinet, Bruce's name was suggested for the honor. This, however, was out of the question, but McKinley reappointed him as register of the treasury. He had held the post only three and a half months when the end came and he succumbed as a victim of diabetes March 17, 1898.[91]

[88] Washington *Post*, January 15, 1884; New York *Times*, November 19, 23, 1884.
[89] Cromwell, *op. cit.*, pp. 169-170.
[90] Charleston *News and Courier*, August 7, 1886.
[91] Cromwell, *op. cit.*, pp. 169-170.

During these later years he had received other honors outside the federal service. He was elected a trustee of Howard University and received the LL.D. degree from this school. Even in the South a kindly feeling had developed for him, if only by contrast with white Republicans, who were hated. An old-time Democratic paper had stated that he was equal in ability to the average cabinet officer of the day and bore a higher character, personally and officially, than ninety per cent of the candidates for prominent positions, that he was cleaner and better in every way than Conkling, Ingersoll, Christiancy, Robeson, and a swarm of lesser lights.[92] He had proved himself personally popular and officially successful. His duties had been well performed and his infectious good humor had disarmed prejudice. As a result there was genuine sorrow at his untimely death. The funeral services at the Metropolitan African Methodist Episcopal Church in Washington were attended by a large throng of both races. Congressmen acted as honorary pallbearers and a tribute by Senator Allison was read. Delegations from all the bureaus of the Treasury Department were present. He was buried in Woodlawn Cemetery, where Langston had been buried a few months before. As Fred Douglass, too, was dead, the Negro race felt that it was indeed bereft. And the feeling among the whites was that Bruce had discharged his duties as well as they could have been done by anyone with his preparation, overshadowed by the partisanship of those troublous years.[93]

[92] Charleston *News and Courier*, January 10, 1881.
[93] New York *Times*, March 18, 1898; Washington *Evening Star*, March 21, 1898; Washington *Post*, March 22, 1898. None of these papers gave front page publicity to his death.

III

THE NEGRO IN THE HOUSE OF REPRESENT-
ATIVES DURING RECONSTRUCTION,
1870-1876

NATURALLY NEGROES had a better chance to be elected to any and all offices while Reconstruction was still in progress and while all the state election machinery was controlled by their political party than they had before or after. Yet we shall see that a number of Negroes were elected to Congress after Reconstruction. It is easily seen that Negro candidacy for the House of Representatives was much more likely to be successful than such candidacy for the Senate. Since voting for senator in the legislature was more or less public, white legislators were averse to casting their ballots for Negro candidates. But in the secret ballot of a general election to the House it seems likely that a considerable number of whites voted for Negro nominees. To what extent this was true is only a matter of speculation, but in some special cases strong inferences may be drawn.

It is proposed to consider the situation by states, beginning with South Carolina and extending southward through Louisiana, and northward through Virginia, as all these states were represented in the House of Representatives by Negroes in time.

SOUTH CAROLINA

Just as Mississippi was conspicuous for having two Negro senators, in like manner was South Carolina outstanding in he number of its Negro representatives. This was to be expected from its large Negro population. In 1860 there were 12,320 blacks to 291,300 whites, while by 1870 the blacks had increased to 415,814 and the whites had actually decreased to 289,667. In the next decade the disproportion became greater, for by 1880 the blacks numbered 604,332 and he whites only 391,105. Accordingly, when the registration f voters was taken in October, 1867, the names of only 6,000 whites were recorded as compared to 79,000 blacks. Only ten counties of the state had a majority of white voters, while twenty-one had Negro majorities. Indeed, in Berkeley he odds were eight to one; in Beaufort, seven to one; in Georgetown, six to one; and even in the capital county of Richland the whites made up less than half the registered voters.[1]

From 1867 to 1870 these Negroes were taking part in local and state politics, preparatory to plunging into national politics. The Republican party in the State was organized at Columbia, July 24, 1867. A state committee was formed, and J. H. Rainey was appointed on it for Georgetown.[2] When the onstitutional convention met in Columbia, January 14, 1868, Negroes were in a majority by seventy-six to forty-eight, although fifty-nine of them were not taxpayers. All six of the Negroes who were soon to serve in Congress were delegates and took an active part. DeLarge was the most prominent of them; Elliott and Cain, almost equally so; while Rainey, Ransier, and Smalls did not have much to say. C. P. Leslie, a white delegate, called DeLarge the best parliamentary tactician on the floor. Yet one who reads the records of the convention is impressed with how much time was wasted on irrelevant matters or on things out of its jurisdic-

---

[1] John S. Reynolds, *Reconstruction in South Carolina, 1865-1877*, p. 13; A. A. Taylor, *The Negro in South Carolina During the Reconstruction*, p. 5.

[2] Reynolds, *op. cit.*, p. 61.

tion and with how often the color issue was obtruded by th Negroes.[3]

Negroes were again prominent in the legislature which me July 6, 1868. There were twenty-one whites to ten Negroe in the Senate but in the House the Negroes predominated b seventy-eight to forty-six.[4] So by the summer of 1870 th stage was set for Negro aspirants to federal office also. Th Democrats were stunned and helpless, and there were ver few white Republicans; consequently ambitious black leader seized the opportunity.

In the proud capital city Robert Brown Elliott was nomi nated for Congress from the third district over S. L. Hoge a white man. DeLarge was named in the second district backed by Cain and Ransier. Rainey was the nominee in th first district. Senator Sawyer had urged the voters to selec men not because they were black but because they were capa ble; however, the Negro voters knew that they supplied th votes, and they insisted on their share of the offices.[5] Six week before the election C. W. Dudley, a white man, was put i the field against Rainey, who had alienated possible conserva tive support by his bitter attacks on the white race. Elliot also was opposed by a white man, J. E. Bacon, who charged Elliott with corruption in many instances, for although at th time of his marriage in Edgefield he did not have money enough to pay his fare to Columbia, and although his presen salary was $3,000, he was now worth $100,000.[6]

When the returns were in on October 19, they proved tha these charges had fallen flat, for all three Negroes were electe over the white Reform candidates. Rainey had almost 9,00 lead, Elliott almost 7,000, while DeLarge's was only 500 t

[3] *Ibid.*, p. 77; *Proceedings of Constitutional Convention of South Carolina passim.*

[4] Reynolds, *op. cit.*, p. 106.

[5] Charleston *Daily Republican*, July 30, 1870.

[6] Charleston *Daily Courier*, September 12, October 11, 1870.

)0 and was contested by C. C. Bowen. It was charged that
ere were gross frauds and that even the Negro women had
ted in place of their husbands.[7]

Elliott and DeLarge were elected to the Forty-second Con-
ess, and Rainey was elected to fill a vacancy in the Forty-
st, becoming then the first Negro member of the House of
epresentatives. While this choice did not create the sensa-
on that Revels' election to the Senate did, Rainey attracted
nsiderable attention and was destined to serve longer in
ongress than any other member of his race—in five sessions,
70-1879.

James Hayne Rainey was born June 21, 1832, at George-
wn, South Carolina. His parents were slaves but bought
eir freedom and were fairly prosperous; his father was a
rber. The son followed the same trade and picked up some
ucation outside the schools. In 1862 he was drafted to work
the Confederate fortifications in Charleston, but soon
caped to the West Indies, where he remained until the close
the war. Rainey was a light mulatto with regular features;
ight, genial eyes; pleasant expression; broad, clear brow;
d a profusion of silky hair. He was of medium height, with
graceful and easy carriage and with very small hands, which
used effectively in gesturing. He was courteous and suave
ther than aggressive, but could defend himself well if neces-
ry. As a speaker he was fluent and even eloquent on occa-
on, moderate but earnest, and he held his own with
ponents even in impromptu debate.[8]

When Congress convened in December, 1870, Rainey ap-
ared and was sworn in. However, he took very little active
rt in this short session. He presented three petitions for the
moval of political disabilities and delivered a memorial of

---

[7] New York *Times,* November 11, 1870; Charleston *Daily Courier,* November
December 2, 1870.
[8] *Cong. Directory,* p. 1440; Marie Le Baron in special to St. Louis *Globe,* April
1874, reprinted in *National Republican,* April 16, 1874.

the National Colored Labor Convention on Southern conditions.[9]

During the Forty-second Congress, which met in March 1871, he became more active and on April 1 made a vigorous speech on legislation to enforce the Fourteenth Amendment, charging that outrages in South Carolina called for some action. Holding that the whites, relying on official leniency, had become bolder and should be repressed, Rainey demanded that the constitutional guarantees be carried out, at the same time deploring any bitterness and asserting he was proud of the prestige of his state.[10]

In the next session he made several speeches on timely subjects, speaking for an appropriation to enforce the Ku Klux Act and in favor of amnesty if joined to civil rights.[11] He presented ten petitions for the passage of the Civil Rights Bill and proposed a bill for the complete removal of all political disabilities.[12]

In the third and final session of this Congress, Rainey introduced a laudable bill to establish an American line of steamships for direct trade with Haiti and for carrying the mail there. However, no action was taken on this.[13]

Rainey's district was so strongly Republican, and he pleased the party so well that he had no opposition in the election of 1872. He received 19,765 votes, which was a large number even considering the lack of opposition.[14]

As a result, he seemed to have acquired new prestige in Congress and to have become more at ease in filling the duties of his office. In the Forty-third Congress he was appointed to the Indian Affairs and Freedmen's Affairs Committees and

9 *Cong. Globe*, 41st Cong., 3rd Sess., pp. 64, 537, 615.

10 *Ibid.*, 42nd Cong., 1st Sess., pp. 5, 339, 393-394.

11 *Ibid.*, 2nd Sess., pp. 1439-1442, 3382.

12 *Ibid.*, pp. 8, 691.

13 *Ibid.*, 3rd Sess., p. 351.

14 *World Almanac*, 1872.

the special committee to attend Sumner's funeral. Also,
when memorial exercises for Sumner were held in the House,
Rainey was the only Negro on the program. Unhappily, he
spoke immediately following the eulogy of Lamar, which
became famous as sounding a note of sectional reconciliation.
Rainey eulogized Sumner well but struck a discordant note
by referring to the regrettable Brooks-Sumner fight.[15] He
continued his advocacy of civil rights but claimed that social
equality was another matter. Negroes, he showed, were
granted all rights in the hotels and restaurants of the East and
of Ohio, but in Washington even Negro congressmen suffered discrimination. In order to show that he meant what he
said, Rainey entered a white hotel dining room in Suffolk,
Virginia, some weeks later and was forcibly ejected.[16]

He displayed a more pleasant phase of his interests when he
made a plea for the support of Forts Moultrie and Sumter
because of their historical associations. The South, in his view,
had been neglected in appropriations. In like vein was his
defense of the Chinese in California. Because they worked for
low wages and did not vote, he protested against their ill
treatment.[17] These two speeches show that he could sometimes
forget alleged abuse of his race, but such nonpartisan mo-
ments were rare.

During this session Rainey received a special honor which
no contemporary of his race enjoyed. While the Indian bill
was under discussion, he was called to the chair to preside over
the House. Although this is a common practice, yet this unusual occupant of the role of Henry Clay caused bold head-
lines in the New York *Herald*—"A Liberated Slave in the
Speaker's Chair." It was only a complimentary gesture, but
the Republicans feared that the Negro vote was wavering and

---

[15] *Cong. Rec.*, 43rd Cong., 1st Sess., pp. 73, 74, 3412.
[16] *Ibid.*, pp. 343, 344; Raleigh *Daily Sentinel*, July 13, 1874.
[17] *Cong. Rec.*, 43rd Cong., 1st Sess., pp. 1442, 1443, 4967.

were doing everything possible to hold the Negroes in lin[e] during the campaign which was opening.[18]

Returning home, he was renominated at Florence, bu[t] Samuel Lee, another Negro, ran also and gave him a clos[e] race, Rainey having a majority of only 800 votes.[19]

In the next session, Rainey delivered his most extende[d] speech in Congress, and it was probably his best. He stoutl[y] insisted on all civil rights for Negroes, but again sought t[o] show that social equality would not result thereby. For h[e] said:

Social equality consists in congeniality of feeling, a reciproci[ty] of sentiment and mutual social recognition among men which [is] graded according to desire and taste and not by any known or po[s]-sible law.... I venture to assert to my white fellow citizens th[at] we, the colored people, are not in quest of social equality. For o[ne] I do not ask to be received into your family circles if you are n[ot] disposed to receive me there. Among my own race we have [as] much respectability, intelligence, virtue and refinement possible t[o] expect from any class circumstanced as we have been.

Rainey favored mixed schools also, thinking they had worke[d] well wherever tried.[20]

The Forty-fourth Congress was Democratic in the Hous[e] but Rainey was treated well in committee assignments. H[e] was a member of the Special Centennial Committee beside[s] being given membership on two regular committees, namel[y] Invalid Pensions and Freedmen's Bank.[21] Soon after Raine[y] was seated, Lee contested his election, but Rainey was n[ot] unseated. The Democratic majority was so large that th[e] Democrats could afford to be generous.[22] In the second sessi[on] of this Congress Rainey and Lee were allowed $1,200 eac[h]

18 Mobile *Register* quoting New York *Herald,* May 7, 1874.

19 Columbia *Union Herald,* September 25, 1874; *World Almanac,* 1875.

20 *Cong. Rec.,* 43rd Cong., 2nd Sess., pp. 958-960.

21 *Ibid.,* 44th Cong., 1st Sess., pp. 250, 251, 330.

22 *Ibid.,* p. 3294.

or the expenses of their contest. But Rainey did not consider imself obligated to the Democratic majority and February 8, 1877, in the last days of Reconstruction, he spoke in defense of the policy that had been pursued in the South, even he use of federal troops at the polls in South Carolina. He prepared a much more extensive speech on the election of 876, but was not permitted to deliver it. Its perusal shows hat he believed the Democrats had resorted to wholesale allot stuffing.[23]

Although Rainey served in Congress after Reconstruction, t is now appropriate to survey his career during Reconstruction. He usually talked vindictively towards the South, but t is doubtful in view of his voting whether he meant what he said. It is not necessary to discuss all of his votes, but a cross section will show his legislative policies. In his first session he favored enforcement of the Fifteenth Amendment and continuation of political disabilities, but he was against prescribing an oath for office.[24] Reviewing a session of the Forty-second Congress we find the same division. He favored the Credit Mobilier investigation, but he voted against condemning Ames and Brooks for their guilt. He wished to refund the cotton tax, but to keep the test oath.[25] In the Forty-third Congress he voted for the completed Civil Rights Bill and for sustaining Kellogg in Louisiana, but he opposed his party's conference tariff report.[26] These votes show that Rainey, in common with other Negro congressmen, adhered, first of all, to his party and then to the interests of his constituents. The Negro representatives could nearly always be depended upon to support anything that was labeled "Republican."

During the greater part of this Congress, Rainey had as

[23] *Ibid.*, pp. 1560, 2015, 2016, Appendix, pp. 217-219.
[24] *Cong. Globe*, 41st Cong., 3rd Sess., pp. 1285, 151, 887.
[25] *Ibid.*, pp. 360, 1833, 891, 541.
[26] *Cong. Rec.*, 43rd Cong., 1st Sess., pp. 1011, 1986, 844.

colleagues DeLarge and Elliott, though the former was unseated and the latter resigned before the end. Robert Carlos
DeLarge was born March 15, 1842, at Aiken. He was self-
educated and had taken an active part in local and state politics, serving in the constitutional convention, and in the legislature, on the sinking fund commission, and as land commissioner. In this last position there was charge of corruption
against him, but the land office already had a bad reputation
when turned over to him by C. P. Leslie, a white man. Consequently, in his campaign for Congress it was said that many
whites voted for him in preference to Bowen, the white candidate.[27]

Partly out of gratitude, no doubt, he early took a stand for
conciliation and removal of political disabilities, though he
wished it coupled with protection of Southern loyalists. He
spoke at length favoring enforcement of the Fourteenth
Amendment, but insisted that the Southerners be restored to
participation in the government. Otherwise, he showed, they
had no incentive in preserving good order. Men should not
act from self-interest but from patriotic interests; and yet men
are only human and act accordingly. DeLarge admitted that
the Republicans were partly to blame for the evils in the
South, but he said Northern men had deceived and misled the
ignorant Negroes.[28] This was one of the sanest and most sensible speeches ever delivered by a Negro congressman.

DeLarge's attention was taken up nearly altogether with
his contest during the next session. At ten different times
papers were received by the House and referred to the committee that was considering the case of Bowen against
DeLarge. Finally on April 20, 1872, he was given indefinite
leave of absence and did not return during the session.[29]

[27] Cong. Directory, p. 896; Taylor, op. cit., pp. 159, 165; Robert Somers,
The Southern States Since the War, 1870-1871, p. 43.

[28] Cong. Globe, 42nd Cong., 1st Sess., Appendix, p. 230.

[29] Ibid., 2nd Sess., pp. 2585, 2594, and passim.

In the third session, also, he took little part aside from his contest. This came to a close when the committee unanimously recommended that DeLarge be ousted but that Bowen not be seated, as there was so much fraud on both sides. This report was adopted by the House January 24, 1873, without a record vote. Rainey and Elliott rallied to his defense but in vain.[30]

This impeached his character, although he was probably no worse than others—just not so careful. A year later, while serving as magistrate in Charleston, he died, and all offices of magistrates closed during the funeral. A large crowd of whites as well as blacks attended the services.[31] A survey of his votes in Congress shows he was not as bitter as some whites. In his last session, while being convicted as a corruptionist, he voted for the Credit Mobilier investigation and for repeal of the test oath.[32]

Robert Brown Elliott, a full-blooded Negro, who also represented South Carolina in the Forty-second Congress, was born in Boston, August 11, 1842. Special correspondence to the St. Louis *Globe* emphasizes the fact that he was a full-blooded Negro, as does also McClure's writings of that time. Elliott's photographs, which are preserved, seem to bear out this fact.[33] He attended High Hollow Academy in England and then graduated from Eton College. He studied law and was admitted to the bar in Columbia, South Carolina, soon thereafter going into politics. From the legislature he was promoted to Congress, never losing contact with party affairs in South Carolina at any time. He was dominant in state

[30] *Ibid.*, 3rd Sess., pp. 689, 842, 845-847.

[31] Charleston *News and Courier*, February 16 and 17, 1874. This is the same paper as the *Daily Courier*. Only the name had changed.

[32] *Cong. Globe*, 42nd Cong., 3rd Sess., pp. 360, 541.

[33] *National Republican*, April 16, 1874, quoting St. Louis *Globe*; Alexander K. McClure, *Recollections of Half a Century*, p. 361. Cromwell, *op. cit.*, p. 47 has pictures of all Negro congressmen.

politics throughout the entire period. All authorities agree in regard to his brilliancy and skill, though his opponents would counterbalance these with grave defects of character.[34]

Here was a man who went through no long period of preparation before making a speech, but within ten days after taking his seat he had spoken at length in favor of political disabilities. Elliott even defended disfranchisement of the Southern whites as being a just penalty. At another time he spoke to the same effect on a bill for enforcement of the Fourteenth Amendment. He argued that such a law would be constitutional and also that it was necessary and just. His quotations from Story and Blackstone showed his legal knowledge, but also revealed his partisanship and bad taste in sneering at Southern chivalry and in using Andersonville conditions to illustrate his point.[35] He urged also an appropriation of $12,000 for the poor in the District of Columbia, who were mostly ex-slaves. He denied that it would put a premium on idleness.[36]

In his next session he was put on the Committee on Education and Labor but was absent much of the time. His main speech was in defense of the state government of South Carolina and its financial policy. He made the best of a very poor case and at that was not very convincing. The whole blame was placed on the Democratic forces of the state for destroying confidence in the state government, thus hurting it in the eyes of Wall Street. He trusted the time would soon come when all his fellow citizens, regardless of nationality, would "recognize the universal fatherhood of God and brotherhood of men." [37] He, at this time, introduced a bill to relieve James D. Treadwell of political disabilities. Before it could pass, a general amnesty bill was put through. Yet he must

[34] *Cong. Directory*, p. 941.
[35] *Cong. Globe*, 42nd Cong., 1st Sess., pp. 102, 389-392.
[36] *Ibid.*, p. 620.
[37] *Ibid.*, 2nd Sess., Appendix, pp. 490-492.

have received credit for good intentions, for this white Democrat became his law partner in Columbia later, and they carried on an extensive and profitable practice.[38] During the summer of 1872 Elliott presided over the Republican State Convention and dictated the nomination of the notorious scalawag, Moses, for governor, over Chamberlain. Charges of bribery were made by both factions, and Elliott admitted that one Negro had been promised $2,000 to support Moses. It ended in a bolters' convention, but the Negroes remained regular for the most part, and Elliott was renominated for Congress.[39]

Returning to Washington in December, he was given leave of absence until after the holidays and returned to plan for greater honors at the hands of his state.[40] He had been reelected in 1872 by a 20,000 majority over weak opposition and considered that the will of the people as expressed in this majority would help his fortunes in Columbia.[41] On December 10 the legislature voted for United States senator for the full term. Patterson, Scott, and Elliott were candidates. As Revels' term had ended, Elliott was ambitious to represent the Negroes in the Senate, and it was rumored in Washington that he had a good chance on account of the state administration, but Patterson had the most money and used it freely with success. He received 90 votes to 33 for Elliott and 7 for Scott. As bad as Elliott was considered by the native whites, a discussion in the *Courier* shows that they would have preferred him to either of his corrupt white opponents. It was felt that Elliott had much influence over the Negroes and

[38] *Ibid.*, p. 2442. The *Union Herald* of Columbia, South Carolina, during 1874 ran a daily advertisement for Elliott and Treadwell, law partners. See also *Vicksburg Times*, April 19, 1874.

[39] Reynolds, *op. cit.*, pp. 222-224; Charleston *News and Courier*, August 23 and 24, 1872.

[40] *Cong. Globe*, 42nd Cong., 3rd Sess., p. 26.

[41] *World Almanac*, 1873.

that the Senate might have had a sobering influence on him.[42]

Evidently disappointed that this higher honor had eluded him, Elliott chose to surrender the lesser, also, in order to give more time to state politics. Therefore in January, 1873 he resigned from Congress and no one succeeded him, the place remaining vacant.[43] The current rumor was that he was preparing to run for governor in 1874. It is true that he and Governor Moses had been political allies, but Moses had misgoverned so outrageously that all who valued their own political lives were prepared to abandon him to his fate.[44] A small incident at this time throws significant light on Elliott' character and the high regard in which his intellectual quali ties were held. The Clariosophic Literary Society at the State University elected him to honorary membership. Now it is true that Negroes were in control of the University, and that this formerly very proud old society had declined somewhat yet his election indicates that he was able to move in intellectual circles, though they may not have been of the highest order. He was always able to descend to the plane of cheap politics and, at the same time, to cater to the better classes In this he had the advantage of most Negroes in politics.[45]

However, while waiting for state affairs to develop, Elliott took his seat in the new, Forty-third, Congress, having been elected again in 1872; he was to distinguish himself in this session even more than in the previous one. He was a member of the Militia Committee and of the Education and Labor Committee and introduced a number of bills and petitions As Elliott was noted for bitter partisanship, it is pleasant to record some deviations from it. He introduced a bill to remit

---

[42] Mobile *Register*, October 27, 1872; Reynolds, *op. cit.*, p. 227; Charleston *News and Courier*, December 11, 1872.

[43] Ben Perley Poore, *The Political Register and Congressional Directory*, p. 189, n. 2.

[44] Charleston *News and Courier*, July 21, 1873.

[45] *Ibid.*, December 24, 1873.

the duty on the chimes of St. Michael's in Charleston, probably the most aristocratic white congregation in the state.
Petitions were presented by him for the relief of the Southern
Methodist Publishing House and for extending belligerent
rights to Cuban patriots.[46]

But his most noted work was his famous speech in behalf
of civil rights. Elliott had a keen sense of the dramatic and
the setting furnished the desired elements. Alexander H.
Stephens had made an able speech opposing the proposed bill.
Elliott had replied for an hour while the day drew to a close,
and at adjournment he held the floor, thus giving him a favorable position for the next day. Also, the public was given due
notice in order to be present.[47]

January 6, 1874, Elliott launched into a two-hour speech
in favor of the bill. He disclaimed any radical motive and
claimed that he was only impelled by a desire for justice. He
traced the history of the Negro, showing how his patriotism
had been shown in all wars. Then he replied to Stephens and
argued on the constitutionality of the bill, contending that it
would simply be carrying out the war amendments. He quoted
from Lieber, Hamilton, and the French Constitution of 1793
to prove the nature of civil rights. He admitted there was a
difference between United States privileges and immunities
and state privileges, but contended that there was no distinction in state rights between races. The state might limit certain rights, but they must be equal. However, he defended
the literacy restrictions of the suffrage in Massachusetts as
being necessary protection against ignorant foreigners. Moreover, he believed that the Slaughter-House decision contained
express recognition of the power of Congress to pass the proposed bill if equal justice were denied in state courts.

One is impressed by the logic and delivery of his speech,

[46] *Cong. Rec.*, 43rd Cong., 1st Sess., pp. 74, 937, 216.
[47] *Ibid.*, p. 386.

but several personal allusions were out of place and in bad taste. While technically observing the rule against personalities, he made it very clear that he was denouncing Beck, Harris, and Stephens, all of whom had opposed the bill. However, because of the intense bitterness of the occasion, these very deviations were acclaimed by his admirers.

His conclusions departed from logic to make an emotional appeal equally effective. He said that the Negro had gained his rights one by one. This, now, was needed as the capstone of the temple of liberty. In fact, the Negro race, like Ruth, had reaped the fields of the white Boaz for two centuries. Now the Negro was at last free, but would never leave the land of his former bondage. He ended with the famous old passage: "Entreat me not to leave thee. . . . The Lord do so to me and more also, if aught but death part thee and me." [48]

As he sat down, congressmen and others crowded around him, and for half an hour he held an informal reception on the floor. The Radicals went wild with joy, and the Associated Press heralded his address over the country. No compliment was considered too extravagant. Butler now claimed him for Massachusetts, and compared him to Adams, Warren, Hancock, Sumner, and Phillips; and if he still were a South Carolinian, he was worthy to rank with Hayne, Rutledge, Calhoun, and McDuffie. On Sumner's death a few weeks later, Elliott was invited to deliver an oration in Faneuil Hall, an invitation that was accepted. His oration on this occasion was also considered of unusual merit. However, the *Courier* unkindly suggested that someone wrote the January speech and insinuated that Sumner was the man.[49]

At this height of his fame we have a careful personal description of him by Marie LeBaron. She places Elliott first

[48] *Ibid.*, pp. 407-410.
[49] Cromwell, *op. cit.*, pp. 183, 185; Simmons, *op. cit.*, p. 469; Wm. H. Ferris, *The African Abroad*, II, 745; *National Republican*, April 16, 1874; Charleston *News and Courier*, September 9, 1874.

mong his race in Congress. "A pure African, thirty-two years
of age, he has all the traits of his race but they are toned down,
efined and not repulsive, and the soul looking through
ightens the shadows that covers them like a flash of sun-
ight." He had full lips, broad nose, white teeth, high sloping
orehead, abundant hair, deep chest, broad shoulders, and
hapely limbs. He wore neat black clothes and altogether pre-
ented an agreeable figure. She said that he wielded a blade
of sarcasm like a knife and seemed to have as his motto: "I am
what I am and I believe in my own nobility." He had one of
the best law and miscellaneous libraries in the state and was
able to read French, German, Spanish, and Latin.[50]

As would be expected, his votes were even more partisan
than most of his black colleagues. He opposed amnesty and
upheld those implicated in the Credit Mobilier affair. He also
favored the retention of the franking privilege.[51]

It may seem odd that with this acclaim still ringing in his
ears, he again resigned in October, 1874—the resignation to
take effect November 1.[52] Already he had plunged deeply into
state politics. On September 16 he had been unanimously
elected chairman of the Republican state committee. He also
was elected to the South Carolina house of representatives and
became Speaker of that house.[53] This position of honor, and
incidentally of profit, he occupied for the next two years. He
practically held the affairs of the state in his hand, for Governor Chamberlain was trying to reform the state and Elliott
was free to control the spoilsmen. On March 28, 1875, the
house voted him a gratuity of $1,000. On December 18, 1875,
the legislature elected a notorious Negro, Whipper, a circuit

---

[50] *National Republican*, April 16, 1874, quoting St. Louis *Globe;* Cromwell,
op. cit., p. 187.

[51] *Cong. Globe*, 42nd Cong., 1st Sess., p. 562; 2nd Sess., p. 4469; 3rd Sess.,
pp. 1833, 1843.

[52] Columbia *Union Herald*, October 24, 1874.

[53] *Ibid.*, September 16 and November 25, 1874.

judge. Elliott pushed the matter and made race loyalty the issue, although he had promised Chamberlain to postpone the election until his return. Early in 1876, F. J. Moses, Sr., was elected to the law professorship in the State University; it was alleged that this was done to keep Elliott out of the office.[54]

But in spite of Elliott's discord with Chamberlain they entered the state convention in 1876 arm in arm. Chamberlain was renominated and Elliott was nominated for attorney-general. This coalition disgusted the Democrats who might have accepted Chamberlain on a Reform ticket. Elliott, however, had become widely known as an unscrupulous and dangerous partisan. Chamberlain is usually considered the ablest and most honest of the carpetbaggers, but he made a fatal mistake in allying with Elliott. In his later years he realized this and admitted it.[55]

Even the editor of the official Republican paper, the *Union Herald*, refused to run Elliott's name as the nominee and resigned as a protest. On the Democratic side the denunciation of the *Courier* is typical of the white sentiment toward him:

There is not a worse or more dangerous and unscrupulous fellow in the state than R. B. Elliott. . . . A relentless foe of economy and reform, capable, vindictive and with no law but his own appetites and passions, R. B. Elliott is the exponent of the lowest and most oppressive form of South Carolina Radicalism.[56]

Elliott went down to defeat with the remainder of the ticket. Yet the Republicans claimed the election and organized

[54] Columbia *Union Herald*, March 28, 1875; Charleston *News and Courier*, December 18, 1875; February 23, 1876; Walter Allen, *Governor Chamberlain's Administration in South Carolina*, pp. 194, 198.

[55] Reynolds, *op. cit.*, pp. 259, 366; *The Atlantic Monthly*, April, 1901; Henry T. Thompson, *Ousting the Carpetbagger*, p. 107, n. 145; Charleston *News and Courier*, September 19, 1876.

[56] *Ibid.*

the legislature which met in December. This "Bayonet Legislature" elected a successor to United States Senator Robertson. Again Elliott aspired to this high position, receiving nineteen votes on the first ballot and four on the second ballot, when Corbin was made the choice.[57] Corbin was not seated, but it would have delighted Elliott to have made the contest. As the Senate was Republican, Elliott would probably have been seated, for he was more aggressive than Corbin.

Still grabbing at every straw, Elliott appeared before the Supreme Court of South Carolina, assuming that he was attorney-general. Hampton displaced Chamberlain, but Elliott retained possession of his office in the Capitol. Finally May 1, 1877, he also yielded to the inevitable, surrendered his office, and by that act put an end to his strenuous and colorful political career. He was still influential in his party, but Republicanism in South Carolina was doomed permanently.[58]

However, for patronage purposes, the party organization was kept together, and Elliott continued as its head; but the magic spell of his eloquence was now broken and he had little heart for the futile role he was playing. In 1878 he presided over the state convention, but little enthusiasm could be aroused. Finally in 1880 he resigned and persuaded the convention to make no fight for state office but only for the electoral ticket. Through the influence of John Sherman, he was appointed a special agent for the Treasury Department with headquarters at Charleston. The Democratic legislature disclosed that Elliott had received $4,000 of state funds fraudulently at one time, and T. J. Mackey branded him as former chieftain of the robber band in the legislature.[59]

His meteoric career now drew to a rapid and inglorious

[57] *Ibid.*, December 13, 1876.
[58] *Ibid.*, February 3, April 17, and May 2, 1877.
[59] *Ibid.*, August 8, 1878, September 1 and 4, 1880.

close. Transferred to New Orleans in 1881, he clashed with Pinchback and Kellogg, the bosses of Republicanism there, and was removed by Arthur. Although he resumed the practice of law, he could not make a success of it under the changed conditions. He picked up a precarious living in the city police courts as an attorney for a time, and on August 9, 1884, he died in poverty.[60]

This is one of the most tragic stories of the Negro race; a splendid intellect, improved by the best training, had been prostituted to the baser things of life, to greed for party advantage, for office, and for gold. It was within his power to have cultivated friendly relations between the races and to have thereby rendered a service to both, but he had chosen the other course—and lost. Space forbids inclusion of the many comments on his career but a few from those who knew him best must suffice. Fred Douglass said: "I have known but one other black man to be compared with Elliott and that was S. R. Ward." Chamberlain stated that "Elliott was the most adroit as well as the ablest Negro in the state." But the *News and Courier* insisted that "there was not a more profligate rascal in the state than this man. He did the Negroes injury instead of credit and yet he was no worse than Blaine." [61] It must be remembered that the scholarly Langston had not then been in politics and that Smalls and Lynch were to win national reputations. Yet, after a mature survey of all Negroes in politics, Woodson, the greatest authority of the race, still thinks Elliott was the most brilliant of all. On the other hand, Reynolds, writing twenty years after Elliott's death, denounced him as utterly corrupt and always on the side of robbers. "His personal character was low and he was very immoral for one of his education and party standing. . . . He

[60] Simmons, *op. cit.*, pp. 471, 472; Ferris, *op. cit.*, II, 746; Charleston *News and Courier*, August 13, 1884.

[61] Simmons, *op. cit.*, p. 472; *The Atlantic Monthly*, April, 1901; Charleston *News and Courier*, August 20, 1884.

must be classed among the worst and very lowest of the reconstruction products." [62]

The next Negro to receive our attention in South Carolina was influential for a decade but was so overshadowed by Elliott that little is remembered concerning him. Alonzo Jacob Ransier was born free in Charleston, January 3, 1834. His ancestry was uncertain, but it seems to have been partly French or Haitian. He received a limited education and at the age of sixteen became shipping clerk for a white merchant. This was a violation of the law, and his employer was fined one cent and costs. This seems an indication that the "terrible black code" was used only in emergency cases and was usually a dead letter. By 1870, when Negroes were entering politics, Ransier already had considerable experience, for as early as 1865 General Sickles appointed him registrar of elections. He had served in the constitutional convention, in the legislature, and as a Grant presidential elector in 1868.[63]

Now that he had served his political apprenticeship, he was ready for broader fields of activity. In July, 1870, he was nominated for lieutenant-governor on the Scott ticket. Stress was laid on the fact that Ransier had a reputation for honesty, regardless of the rest of the ticket. The Democrats ran General M. C. Butler against him, but Ransier was elected by 33,000 majority.[64] This state administration was notorious for its extravagance and corruption, yet Ransier came through with a better reputation than most of the participants. But by 1872 the star of Elliott had risen, and he took from Ransier control of the party in the state. There was much political unrest in 1872, and Sumner was trying to carry the Negro

[62] Reynolds, op. cit., p. 286. The author interviewed Dr. C. G. Woodson in November, 1929.

[63] Cong. Directory, p. 1444; W. H. Barnes, The American Government. History of the Forty-third Congress (hereinafter cited History of Forty-third Congress), p. 275; Reynolds, op. cit., pp. 77, 102, 107.

[64] Ibid., p. 147; Charleston Daily Republican, July 28, 1870.

vote for Greeley. Ransier issued an open letter to Pinchback, contending that all Negroes should remain loyal to the party. This no doubt caused his nomination for Congress from the second district in August, 1872. General William Gurney, a Union veteran, opposed him as an Independent Republican, but Ransier had over 13,000 majority.[65]

Ransier had as colleagues in this Congress Rainey, Cain, and Elliott. Consequently, there was not much chance for him to distinguish himself. Being a member of the Manufactures Committee, he proposed some minor bills and presented a number of claims and petitions; but he was entirely unsuccessful in securing action on them. On the very day that Elliott started his famous speech, Ransier tried to make some impression on the House but was decisively rebuffed. Harris had stated that no gentleman on the floor could honestly say that a colored man was created his equal. Ransier: "I can." Harris: "Of course you can; but I am speaking to the white men of the House, and Mr. Speaker, I do not wish to be interrupted again by him." Harris then quoted Lincoln to prove the inequality of the races. Ransier: "I deny that." Harris: "I do not allow you to interrupt me. Sit down; I am talking to white men; I am talking to gentlemen." [66] This was a rather rough introduction for Ransier as it was the first time he had spoken and even then he had not been recognized by the chair. During this trying thirty year period, Southern congressmen often harshly criticized the Negro race and were as harshly answered by the Negro representatives; but the personal interchange of Harris and Ransier was the most disagreeable of all, for up to this time personalities were usually in the background.

But not to be discouraged by this rebuke, Ransier within a few weeks delivered a long, carefully prepared speech in sup-

[65] Barnes, *History of Forty-third Congress*, p. 276.
[66] *Cong. Rec.*, 43rd Cong., 1st Sess., pp. 71, 345, 589, 763, 927.

port of civil rights. He quoted from Negro conventions to show that they favored it and also that the Democrats in the South Carolina legislature did. This bill, he contended, would not cause strife but would bring about harmonious racial relations. The Negro, he said, had done his part in the war and had lost as heavily in proportion as the whites; and he also claimed that the medical examinations showed the Negro to be equally as good military material. Ransier even urged mixed schools and justified them by citing good results at Yale, Harvard, Oberlin, Cornell, Wilberforce, Berea, and Maryville. He closed by trying to prove that it was the Negro vote that had elected Grant in 1872 and, therefore, that this proposed bill would help to reward the race for its party loyalty.[67]

He returned to the same subject near the close of the session and especially stressed the need of civil rights as a debt of gratitude for voting the Republican ticket. He admitted the defects in the state governments of South Carolina, Arkansas, and Louisiana, but held that it did not excuse denial of equal rights to a whole race. "Let justice," he said, "be done though the heavens fall." [68]

Ransier spoke in happier vein in his defense of appropriations for Forts Moultrie and Sumter, showing that in war and peace these were strategic forts and should be maintained.[69]

Ransier was a member of the group which Miss LeBaron analyzed so well for the St. Louis *Globe*. She pictured him as having a look of great courage and sagacity. He was middle-aged, stout, and clumsily built; he moved and spoke uneasily at first but warmed up to fluency and ease. To prove the last quality she recalled that he spoke to a convention of five hun-

[67] *Ibid.*, pp. 1311-1314.
[68] *Ibid.*, p. 1486.
[69] *Ibid.*, p. 1444.

dred women and did not quail. He was known, she said, as a zealous partisan and since 1865 had been active in the equal rights movement.[70]

Ransier returned home in the summer of 1874 and threw himself into the movement to reform the party. He repudiated Moses and warned the Negroes that they must have good government or the suffrage might be qualified. But now, after a long succession of political triumphs, C. W. Buttz, a white man, defeated him for the nomination to Congress. Ransier complained that Buttz used $4,000 to defeat him, but he did not bolt the ticket.[71]

His second and last session of Congress was uneventful. No legislation of importance was initiated or supported by him actively. Ineffectively he tried to obtain funds for the improvement of Charleston harbor. He voted for repeal of the salary increase and for the tariff, and for changing the presidential term to one of six years with no re-election.[72]

He returned to Charleston and became a day laborer for the city government and died August 17, 1882. The comment of the *News and Courier* is brief but significant: "Probably he was the least objectionable Negro who attained high position in the state. . . . For several years he has been in abject poverty and his death is doubtless a release."[73] He had fallen as low as Elliott and yet he had never risen so high.

The next member of the South Carolina group was a case of a "preacher in politics" to the "nth degree," or a "Bishop Cannon of the 70's." Richard Harvey Cain was born April 12, 1825, in Greenbrier County, Virginia. Although he was free born and had no white blood, he had strong racial feeling. (Usually the mulatto and the former slave were more bitter

---

[70] *National Republican* of April 16, 1874, quoting St. Louis *Globe*.

[71] Columbia *Union Herald*, March 11, July 29, August 8 and 21, and September 24, 1874.

[72] *Cong. Rec.*, 43rd Cong., 1st Sess., p. 290; 2nd Sess., pp. 386, 644, 760.

[73] August 18, 1882.

than the full-blooded freedman.) When Cain was only six years of age, his father carried him to Ohio, and he did not return South until the end of the war. Because of this, he was usually regarded in the South as a "Northern man." [74]

He was licensed to preach in the Methodist Episcopal Church but soon changed to the African Methodist Episcopal. After serving as pastor in Missouri and Iowa, he attended Wilberforce University for one year and then preached in Brooklyn during the war years. At the close of the war he was sent to South Carolina, where he was very successful in "missionary" work among the freedmen. Yet he had time to publish a newspaper, the *Missionary Record*, and to take an active part in state politics. In rapid succession he served as alderman in Charleston, member of the constitutional convention, member of the state legislature, and as active campaign orator for Moses in his race for the governorship. During this political experience he received the nickname of "Daddy Cain," which was used in derision by the whites and in respect by the Negroes. [75]

By 1872, Cain was capable of a broader role in politics. He was nominated for congressman-at-large, and this compelled him to support the state administration in all its rottenness. This reveals a fatal weakness in Cain, for he had been outspoken against the thefts of Governor Scott and Speaker Moses; now he joined forces with them and condoned their crimes. His amazing explanation was that if Moses had issued fraudulent pay certificates they were for the benefit of poor Republicans. Naturally, he was elected by an overwhelming majority over his Independent Republican opponent. [76]

One could expect little constructive work in Congress from

---

[74] *Cong. Directory*, p. 774; Reynolds, *op. cit.*, p. 109.

[75] *Dictionary of American Biography*, ed. Allen Johnson and Dumas Malone, III, 403, 404; Reynolds, *op. cit.*, pp. 109, 110.

[76] Charleston *News and Courier*, March 19, May 7, August 23 and 26, 1872; *World Almanac*, 1873.

such a frank partisan. The only bill which he introduced for the interest of his state was one proposing the establishment of a navy yard at Port Royal. He was on the Agriculture Committee but was more interested in civil rights than in everything else combined. January 10, 1874, he delivered an able defense of the proposed bill, but Elliott's noted speech of four days before had covered practically the same ground. Cain again dwelt on the war services of the Negroes and considered that bestowing civil rights would only be an act of justice. He claimed that even mixed schools would work no harm, as South Carolina University had not suffered. If sincere, his attitude would have been commendable when he said: "I want to shake hands over the bloody chasm. . . . I desire to bury the tomahawk forever." [77]

Cain considered himself an authority on educational conditions and was fond of making speeches and citing statistics, often in a reckless manner. This was illustrated when he declared that there was twelve per cent more illiteracy among Southern whites than among the Negroes and that illiteracy in North Carolina amounted to sixty per cent. He admitted he was quoting from memory, and very naturally, he was in great error. This recklessness was again evidenced in his claim that Hannibal, Hanno, Hamilcar, and Euclid were Negroes, simply because they lived in Africa.[78] In the second session he became even more careless in his speech and in his use of statistics. He said: "There is more ignorance in proportion in this country among the whites than there is among the colored." This was an absurd statement on the face of it, illustrating his weakness for opinion unsupported by proof.

Probably his most sensational statement was the expression of his hope that the time would come "when there should be no white, no black . . . but one common brotherhood and one

[77] *Cong. Rec.*, 43rd Cong., 1st Sess., pp. 74, 346, 565-567.
[78] *Ibid.*, pp. 901-903.

united people, going forward forever in the progress of nations." [79]

His votes on great issues showed him always on the side of the administration. He voted against impeaching the notorious Judge Durell, and for the tariff, civil rights, and the support of the Kellogg carpetbag government in Louisiana.[80]

In 1874, Cain joined the reform element in South Carolina and really did some good work in the campaign, in behalf of Judge Green for Governor. But the main faction of the party was too strong, or Cain was distrusted as a reformer, and he was defeated for Congress by a white carpetbagger. Indeed, there were serious reports that he was a swindler on a large scale. He had sold off a large tract of land in small lots, and it was charged that he did not pay for the land. His accuser was a political rival, C. W. Buttz, a white man, and so the charges must be somewhat discounted.[81]

Miss LeBaron's sketch of him at this time is of interest. She noted that he was an African in looks, eloquence, wit, and dramatic power. His long arms waved, and his face assumed in turn a pathetic, humorous, or sardonic expression. Some facetiously called him "the Darwinian missing link." [82] His later career will be related in the next chapter.

The last member of this South Carolina group is in some ways the most remarkable, for he served almost as long as Rainey, and his influence over his race lasted much longer. Robert Smalls was born at Beaufort, South Carolina, April 5, 1839; moved to Charleston, 1851; rose to the rank of captain in the United States Navy and served until 1866. Then he had the usual experience in politics of working up through the lower offices. From 1868 to 1872 he was in the constitu-

[79] *Ibid.*, 2nd Sess., pp. 956, 957, 1151-1153.

[80] *Ibid.*, pp. 324, 644, 1011, 1986.

[81] Taylor, *op. cit.*, p. 211; Charleston *News and Courier*, June 17 and 18, and November 4, 1874.

[82] *National Republican*, April 16, 1874, quoting St. Louis *Globe*.

tional convention or the legislature; and in 1872 he was a delegate to the Republican National Convention.[83] His record for honesty was not good during this period, but disclosures were not made until much later.

During the Republican split in South Carolina, Smalls was a staunch regular and canvassed the state for the whole ticket. He had little trouble in being elected to Congress over J. P. M. Epping, Reform candidate in the third district.[84] Reformers in the state would have to wait for several years.

Smalls was appointed to the Agriculture Committee but presented no agricultural bills, except one to extend time for redemption of lands held for direct taxes. Smalls was not noted for his speaking ability, since he was not well educated and was diffident at first. By nature he was more adapted to the rough-and-tumble campaign than to the sober debates in Congress. It required the stimulus of the 1876 state campaign in South Carolina to induce him to make a speech. Then he asked that no troops be taken from South Carolina for service on the Texas frontier. He blamed the Hamburg riot on the whites and had an anonymous letter read to prove it. Smalls would not reveal the writer of the letter, although he knew, and this gave the wit of the House, S. S. Cox, an opening. Smalls might vouch for the letter, but who vouched for Smalls? Smalls was equal to the occasion and replied, "A majority of 13,000." [85]

Indeed, Smalls was better in repartee than he was in delivering a set speech. This was shown well in his argument with Cox concerning the rottenness of their respective home governments, state and municipal. Cox had quoted extensively from Pike's *The Prostrate State* when Smalls asked if Cox

[83] *Cong. Directory*, p. 1532. Smalls was impressed into the Confederate Navy but took the Confederate ship "Planter" over to the Federal forces and was promoted from pilot to captain.

[84] Columbia *Union Herald*, October 2, 1874; *World Almanac*, 1875.

[85] *Cong. Rec.*, 44th Cong., 1st Sess., pp. 250, 4857, 4641-4643.

had the book of the city of New York. His interchange with Hooker was more bitter, for Hooker asserted that the master class was the Negro's best friend, and Smalls contradicted him. Hooker replied sharply: "Take your seat now. I do not want to be interrupted any further." Smalls still insisted that Negroes never voted with the Southern whites unless coerced by the Ku Klux.[86]

However, not all of his pleas were radical in nature. His support of Port Royal as a naval rendezvous was effective, and he also secured an appropriation for improving the harbor.[87]

It was a pleasure for him to plunge into the bitter state campaign of 1876. He was active in the state and national conventions and in the strenuous canvass which followed. The Democrats elected their state ticket, but the Republicans with the aid of federal troops organized the legislature. Smalls received a vote for the United States Senate, but Elliott was the real choice of the Negroes. Smalls survived the Democratic victory and was re-elected to Congress, but by a scant margin of 1,000 votes.[88]

The short session of Congress, 1876-1877, was practically consumed in discussion of the election of 1876. Everybody wanted to make a speech; and, therefore, Smalls prepared a long, partisan argument, attempting to place all the blame in the South Carolina election on the Democrats. Even for a campaign document some of his charges were ridiculous, such as the one that 25,000 Georgians crossed into South Carolina and voted. At any rate, his speech was not delivered because too many other members were anxious to go on record and crowded him out.[89]

[86] *Ibid.*, pp. 4605-4607, 5384.
[87] *Ibid.*, pp. 3273, 4083.
[88] Reynolds, *op. cit.*, pp. 362, 366; *World Almanac*, 1877; Charleston *News and Courier*, December 13, 1876.
[89] *Cong. Rec.*, 44th Cong., 2nd Sess., Appendix, pp. 123-136.

NORTH CAROLINA

The racial situation in North Carolina was very different from that in South Carolina. There was never any probability of the Negroes controlling North Carolina, and within the Republican party the native white element was always strong. But because of the concentration of the Negroes in the east, they were quite a problem in Congressional and local elections. In fact, there were Negroes in the legislature from 1868 to 1899 inclusive, although they never formed more than a fifth of the number of legislators.[90]

The first Negro to represent North Carolina in Congress was John Adams Hyman. He was born July 23, 1840, near Warrenton. He was sold and sent to Alabama, but returned to North Carolina when emancipated in 1865. Hyman at this time received an elementary education, while he farmed for a living. Consequently, by 1868 he felt capable of engaging in politics. His part in the Constitutional Convention of 1868 was a minor one but immediately afterward he became a member of the legislature and served until 1874. Hyman's native ability was only moderate, but he was willing to carry out the wishes of the "ring." Time after time he was mixed up in questionable or outright corrupt transactions.[91]

Throughout the nation 1874 was a reform year, but the Negroes of the second district of North Carolina were ignorant of that fact. The white Republicans feared the result of putting up Negroes for office, but in the district convention the blacks controlled and insisted on one of their race as the nominee for Congress. Hyman's previous record helped instead of hurt him, and he was nominated and elected by a

[90] Monroe N. Work, comp., "Some Negro Members of Reconstruction Conventions and Legislatures and of Congress," *Journal of Negro History*, V, 75; *Cong. Directory*, p. 1136.

[91] J. G. de R. Hamilton, *Reconstruction in North Carolina*, pp. 368, 380, 386, 431.

large majority. The New York *Herald* remarked that Hyman had been sold seven times and would be sold more times than that while in Congress. The *Herald* evidently did not know that he was able to take care of himself in this respect, and that if any selling were done he would get the money this time.[92]

As this Forty-fourth Congress was Democratic, and as Hyman was inexperienced, he was placed on the Manufactures Committee and had little to say. Although he presented a number of private claims and petitions, none of them received any consideration. The same fate awaited his bills of a more public nature: to reimburse Jones County for its courthouse, destroyed by Federal troops; to erect a lighthouse on Pamlico Sound; and to give relief to the western Cherokees.[93]

Before the long session adjourned, Hyman had already failed of renomination. This was partly due to the desire of the North Carolina Republicans to subordinate the Negroes in the state, and partly due to Hyman's own personal faults. He had overdrawn his salary and made debts in Washington and Baltimore which he could not meet. James Harris and other Negro leaders supported him in the convention, and he led at first, but Governor Brogden was finally nominated.[94]

During the next session of Congress, Hyman introduced a private bill but made no remarks of any kind. But he voted against the electoral commission, against investigation of the Louisiana returning board, and against investigation of the coercion of federal employees. Although the party had deserted him, he was loyal to it to the last.[95]

Such is the brief story of as futile a term of office as ever was served in the American Congress. Even the Negroes were

[92] *Ibid.*, pp. 601-603; Raleigh *Sentinel*, September 22, 1874, quoting New York *Herald.*

[93] *Cong. Rec.*, 44th Cong., 1st Sess., pp. 250, 271, 588, 3120, 3340.

[94] Hamilton, *op. cit.*, p. 647; Raleigh *Sentinel*, July 27 and 28, 1876.

[95] *Cong. Rec.*, 44th Cong., 2nd Sess., pp. 132, 1050, 1071, 1302.

content for six years to have a white man represent them from this district. Hyman was not the material of which capable congressmen were made, yet even he could be superior in some ways to Douglass, the idol of the race. Douglass spoke at Warrenton in 1872, and for the occasion Hyman had placed a glass of wine on the speaker's table. Douglass sipped it and was so discourteous as to say that the sherry might have been worse but he was puzzled to see how. Hyman remarked: "Mr. Douglass's manners—what he has—may be good enough for his Northern friends but they don't set well with folks who know what manners is." [96] Hyman was given a very minor place in the federal revenue service for a year. Then he passed into obscurity which lasted until his death in Washington, September 14, 1891.[97]

Georgia

Georgia had a large Negro population, but the Negroes were not so aggressive in politics as they were in the Carolinas. On the other hand, they permitted the white Republicans to control the party machinery and to secure most of the offices. In 1870 it was estimated that Negroes composed ninety-eight per cent of the party, but they were given the short term nomination in every case.[98]

In accordance with this policy Long was nominated in the fourth district convention at Macon, while T. J. Speer, a white man, was given the long term nomination. Both were nominated by acclamation and with enthusiasm. Long made a series of speeches over the district ending in his home city the night before election. In this address he threatened the Negroes with social and religious ostracism unless they voted

[96] Wilson, *op. cit.*, p. 85.
[97] *Cong. Directory*, p. 1136.
[98] Savannah *Republican*, October 8, 1870.

the Republican ticket. Probably as a result, there was a serious race riot at Macon on December 20, election day. This peculiar special election was conducted for three days, giving plenty of chance for "plural" voting. It was suspected that Alabama and South Carolina Negroes crossed the line and took advantage of the situation. At any rate, Long carried Bibb, his home county, by a majority of fifty-one and the district by a majority of nine hundred over Lawton, the Democrat.[99]

Jefferson Franklin Long was born March 3, 1836, near Knoxville, Georgia. He was self-educated and became a merchant tailor in Macon. Although by December 22 his election was certain, yet it was January 16, 1871, before he was sworn in, due to the tangle over Georgia's readmission. He was warmly welcomed by the white Republicans and also by Rainey. It was said that Long was not as light a mulatto as Rainey, and therefore was more representative of the race, and also that he was an intelligent looking man.[100]

February 1, 1871, Long made the first speech of a Negro member in the House. Rainey had been a member for over a month but had never made a speech. A bill was before the House proposing to modify the test oath. Long spoke in opposition to the bill, as he feared that leniency to Southern whites was a mistaken policy. He charged that already fifty-five loyalists had been shot down in Georgia, and no one had been punished. The Ku Klux Klan, he alleged, controlled even judges and jurors. He expressed goodwill for the law-abiding element but would support no modification for the disloyal. This short speech was the only one Long delivered, as his term expired March 4. The New York *Tribune* was very favorably impressed. "In manner he was perfectly self-

[99] Atlanta *New Era*, October 6 and December 1, 1870; Savannah *Republican*, December 22 and 24, 1870; Barnes, *History of Forty-first Congress*, p. 325.
[100] *Cong. Directory*, p. 1236; Savannah *Republican*, January 20, 1871; Charleston *Daily Courier*, January 20, 1871.

possessed. His voice is full and powerful, filling the Hall with ease while his enunciation was quite good." But his home paper was not so complimentary. "Long embraced the chance to speak against amnesty and let off his budget of lies with which he went freighted to Washington." [101]

The few votes which he had an opportunity to cast were largely partisan. These included support of enforcement of the Fifteenth Amendment, of universal suffrage in the District of Columbia, and of unseating S. A. Corker, the Georgia Democrat, whose seat was claimed by another Negro, T. P. Beard. [102]

Long resumed his business in Macon and did not hold public office again, although he was still interested in politics. He was prominent in 1874 in a Southern Republican convention at Chattanooga, and in 1880 was a delegate to the Republican National Convention. He died at Macon, February 5, 1900.

He was the only Negro ever to represent Georgia in Congress and his influence was so slight that Wooley and Thompson in their histories of Reconstruction in Georgia do not even mention his name. The races understand each other better in Georgia than in some other states. The small farm prevailed more, and even on the plantations the white owner was more in contact with the Negro tenant; a friendly relationship resulted. [103]

FLORIDA

In Florida there was a racial situation somewhat like the one in Georgia. The Negroes, in a strong minority in the

[101] *Cong. Globe,* 41st Cong., 3rd Sess., pp. 881, 882; Atlanta *New Era,* February 9, 1871, quoting New York *Tribune;* Savannah *Republican,* February 5, 1871.

[102] *Cong. Globe,* 41st Cong., 3rd Sess., pp. 646, 707, 1285.

[103] *Cong. Directory,* p. 1236; New Orleans *Times,* October 14, and 16, 1874; James Ford Rhodes, *History of the United States from the Compromise of 1850,* VI, 255, 258.

state, formed about ninety-five per cent of the Republican party. Yet only one Negro ever represented the state in Congress, owing to the machinations of the carpetbaggers to keep all the offices in their hands. Indeed, it sometimes appeared that the carpetbaggers preferred a Democrat to a Negro and worked secretly to defeat their own, unwelcome nominee. Consequently, even in the state legislature the Negroes were never numerous.[104]

Such dissensions were disclosed in 1870 at the state convention. The Negroes made an open issue and insisted that the carpetbag incumbent withdraw in favor of a Negro for Congress. This was done and Walls was nominated. The carpetbag "ring," smarting under its rebuff, tried to elect its lieutenant-governor and to let Walls be beaten by the Democrat. However, both Democrats were elected and the machine was puzzled how to count in its man but to leave Walls out. The board of canvassers solved it by counting in both Republicans, and rejecting outright the total votes of nine Democratic counties.[105]

Josiah Thomas Walls was born in Winchester, Virginia, December 30, 1842. He was a free Negro but was pressed into Confederate service as servant to an artillery battery. Having been captured at Yorktown, he was carried to Harrisburg, Pennsylvania, where he attended school a year. Then in 1863 he entered the Federal army as a private, but by efficient work he rose to be sergeant major and instructor of artillery. Settling in Florida at the close of the war, he farmed and entered state politics through the constitutional convention and legislature.[106]

Before the reapportionment based on the census of 1870,

104 Work, "Some Negro Members . . . of Congress," *Journal of Negro History*, V, 69.
105 William W. Davis, *The Civil War and Reconstruction in Florida*, pp. 618, 627.
106 *Cong. Directory*, p. 1662; Barnes, *History of Forty-third Congress*, p. 215.

Florida had only one member of the House of Representatives. From 1872 on, she has had two or more. Therefore, Walls had the unique distinction of representing the whole state, an honor which no other Negro has had. He was not well equipped to understand the many important issues of the day, but at least he made a sincere effort to carry out his duties and did so remarkably well, considering his limitations. Walls was a Negro first, and a Republican next, as were all Negro congressmen of this study, but he did not stop with those two ideals, as most of his race did. It is notable how many bills he introduced for the welfare of his constituents and state as a whole. To be sure, most of these failed to pass, but they were commendable, at any rate. He, like others, favored the policy of equal rights and general amnesty, and proposed a bill to this effect.[107]

His first extended speech showed his naïve faith in education as a panacea. He advocated a National Educational Fund and said: "Education is the panacea for all our social evils, injustices, and oppressions." He feared that if education were left to the Southern states, they would neglect it.[108]

Silas Niblack had contested Walls's election from the first, but Congress dragged it out in committee until near the close of this Congress. Finally, January 29, 1873, the contest was laid before the House, and without a record vote Walls was unseated.[109]

By 1872, the state had been divided into two districts, and the Negroes insisted on having the second, or northern, district. Walls was renominated, and, as the Democrats were demoralized, he won a clear title this time with 1,700 majority. Even with a colleague to take care of the interests of

[107] *Cong. Globe,* 42nd Cong., 1st Sess., pp. 79, 178; 2nd Sess., pp. 198, 683; 3rd Sess., p. 220. These concerned public buildings, coastal defense, and grant of public lands, for the most part.

[108] *Ibid.,* 2nd Sess., pp. 808-810.

[109] *Ibid.,* 3rd Sess., p. 949.

the state, Walls introduced twenty bills in the first session of the new Congress. A significant one proposed to grant belligerent rights to the insurgent Cubans. Walls's view was that Spain's emancipation act was a delusion and that 500,000 Negroes were still in slavery in Cuba. Other interests of his were: relief of Seminole War veterans, improvement of harbors, granting of public lands to Florida railroads.[110] Some remarks on the floor proved that Walls was a Florida "booster," much like the present day variety. He claimed that "my own sunny state" had a thousand rare and valuable inducements to immigration.[111]

Miss LeBaron included Walls in her revealing analysis of the seven Negroes of the Forty-third Congress. She described him as a good writer but not a good speaker; an effective and tireless worker; tactful, foresighted, and practical.[112]

In 1874, Walls again had a factional fight on his hands in Florida. In the district convention, he was renominated easily and the *New South* supported him heartily, but Governor Stearns's paper, the *Florida Union*, attacked him, even after his nomination. "And so Mr. Walls as a common citizen is worthy of commendation but as a Congressman, he is far beneath what our necessities demand." To divide the Negro vote, the machine suggested other Negroes instead of Walls. Walls must have felt that he must look to his own election, for lawless practices were resorted to in his home county. Again the state board of canvassers declared him elected. It seems that the carpetbaggers fought him up to election day and then, for the sake of party gain, were willing to help him.[113]

Walls returned to a Democratic House in December, 1875.

110 Davis, *op. cit.*, p. 638, n. 1; *Cong. Rec.*, 43rd Cong., 1st Sess., pp. 87, 88, 206, Appendix, p. 27.
111 *Ibid.*, Appendix, p. 250.
112 *National Republican*, April 16, 1874, quoting St. Louis *Globe*.
113 Davis, *op. cit.*, p. 642; Jacksonville *New South*, August 12 and 26, 1874.

He was made a member of the nominal Mileage Committee, and his bills received scant attention; yet he introduced a number, as usual. J. J. Finley was contesting his seat and, after a long-drawn-out dispute, Walls was unseated April 19, 1876. This is an unenviable distinction which he achieved— that of being twice unseated.[114]

By a deal between J. R. Scott and Horatio Bisbee, Bisbee received the nomination over Walls in 1876. The ring tried to salve Walls's feelings a bit by making him a member of the executive committee; he, however, took no active part in the state campaign. Nevertheless, at the close, since Walls was again a member of the legislature, he did help Zach Chandler capture Florida's electoral vote for Hayes. Strange as it may seem, he received no reward for this but returned to farming. When he was ruined financially by the frost killing his orange trees, he became superintendent of the farm at the Tallahassee State College. There he lived until his death May 5, 1905.[115]

ALABAMA

Beginning with 1868, a considerable number of Negroes served in the Alabama legislature, but, not satisfied, they wished their share of the higher offices. It was estimated that the Negroes furnished 90,000 votes in the Republican party, but the whites, with only 10,000 votes, held all major offices. The Democratic press urged the Negroes to assert themselves as they did in South Carolina, and then with sharp inconsistency severely assailed any Negro who followed this advice. In fact, the main Democratic organ, the Mobile *Register*, announced itself as a white man's paper, dedicated to a white man's party, government, and state.[116]

[114] *Cong. Rec.*, 44th Cong., 1st Sess., pp. 251, 295, 2602.
[115] John Wallace, *Carpet-bag Rule in Florida*, pp. 126, 133, 301, 332; Jacksonville *Florida Union*, August 17, 1876; Ferris, *op. cit.*, II, 761, 762.
[116] Mobile *Register*, July 1 and 3, 1870.

When the Republican state convention met in September, 1870, the white Secretary of State withdrew to give the Negroes a place on the state ticket, and Rapier was nominated by acclamation. In like manner, the district convention in the "Black Belt," meeting at Selma, unanimously nominated Turner for Congress from this first district. Three carpetbaggers wanted the nomination and talked of another convention but took no action. Naturally the Negroes were jubilant, and Turner in his campaign attacked the carpetbaggers openly and by name. He said they had not helped him either with speeches or funds, and that he was compelled to sell a horse to pay his canvassing expenses. This dissension probably defeated Rapier, but Turner was elected by a large majority.[117]

Benjamin Sterling Turner was born March 17, 1825, near Weldon, North Carolina. He was carried to Alabama as a slave and remained there until emancipation. He had served as tax collector of Dallas County and as councilman of the city of Selma. By running a livery stable, he had amassed considerable wealth, and was popular with the native whites. Yet his education was very scanty, and it was reported that he could write his name and nothing more.[118]

During the first session of Congress, Turner was inarticulate. He introduced only three bills and none of them received any consideration. One of these was commendable in that it proposed the removal of all political and legal disabilities, but this was not original with him.[119]

In the next session, however, Turner was more at ease on the floor of the House. Indeed, he felt experienced enough to rise to a point of order in which he was sustained by the chair. He was given leave to print two very able speeches,

[117] Montgomery *Alabama Journal*, September 2 and 22, 1870; Mobile *Register*, October 25, 1870; *World Almanac*, 1871.
[118] *Cong. Directory*, p. 1631; Mobile *Register*, December, 15, 1870.
[119] *Cong. Globe*, 42nd Cong., 1st Sess., pp. 559, 732, 835.

favoring refund of the cotton tax, and asking for public buildings in Selma. In reference to the cotton tax, he showed that it was unconstitutional and that the South had lost $250,-000,000 as a result. He proposed as partial compensation that public lands be sold in small tracts, on easy terms to the purchaser. These bills did not pass; but he secured the passage of two private pension bills.[120]

On account of his defeat in 1872, Turner seemed to lose interest in his final session—that of December to March, 1872-1873. But as the New York *Tribune* said, he was always present and always voted right, under Benjamin Butler's direction. His party loyalty had caused him to support the test oath, mixed schools, civil rights, and the franking privilege; and he had opposed civil service reform, expulsion of Ames and Brooks, and removal of names of battles on the war flags.[121]

Turner secured renomination in 1872, but Philip Joseph, another Negro, bolted the party and ran also. The Democrats and Liberal Republicans united on F. G. Bromberg and elected him, owing to the Republican split. Turner continued in county politics, but J. T. Rapier and Jeremiah Haralson had replaced him as leaders of the race. He resumed his farming and continued it until his death March 21, 1894.[122]

The next Negro to represent Alabama in Congress was of a different type altogether. James Thomas Rapier was born November 13, 1837, at Florence, Alabama. His father was free and wealthy, so that he could afford a tutor for his son and then an education for him in Canada. Rapier studied law, was admitted to the bar, but never practiced. Returning to Alabama in 1865, he became a successful cotton planter. He

---

[120] *Ibid.*, 2nd Sess., pp. 2715, 3850, Appendix, pp. 530, 540.

[121] New York *Tribune*, September 24, 1872; *Cong. Globe*, 42nd Cong., 2nd Sess., pp. 1117, 4469, 2585; 3rd Sess., pp. 221, 541, 1833.

[122] New York *Times*, November 7, 1872; *Cong. Directory*, p. 1631.

was also active in state politics, but was defeated in 1870 for
Secretary of State. However, in 1872 he easily won the con-
gressional nomination in the second district and defeated his
Democratic opponent by a safe majority.[123]

In the Forty-third Congress, Rapier was a member of the
Education and Labor Committee, but he was more interested
in civil rights than anything else. His eight years residence
in Canada had given him an intense resentment of any discrimination against his race. He was partly of French stock,
had represented the United States at the World's Fair in
Paris, and had been Alabama's commissioner to the Vienna
Exposition. All these things combined to kindle his wrath
against the racial restrictions and prejudices which he saw
around him.[124]

Elliott was more widely known and was a better speaker
than Rapier, but Rapier's speech on civil rights is more readable than Elliott's. He had a gift of vividness, secured partly
by the use of incidents and by naming definite persons. The
Negro was between Scylla and Charybdis: if he favored the
bill he was charged with favoring social equality; if he opposed it, he was accused of a lack of interest in what concerned
him so closely. Rapier showed the anomaly of his privileged
position in Congress, though he now was refused a meal at
every inn from Washington to Montgomery. He said that
at one time humanity imposed on the Jew, but that it now
imposed on the Negro. Yet he charged this superior race
with gross inconsistency. The whites, he said, turned up their
noses at a Negro man but cohabited with Negro women.
Rapier stated his position decisively: "Nothing short of a complete acknowledgement of my manhood will satisfy me. I have
no compromises to make and shall unwillingly accept any." [125]

[123] *Ibid.*, p. 1445; New York *Times*, November 7, 1872.
[124] *Cong. Rec.*, 43rd Cong., 1st Sess., p. 74.
[125] *Ibid.*

In the next session he returned to the same subject and insisted not only on equal rights but on community of enjoyment, instead of separate enjoyment as suggested by Alex White, a white Republican congressman from Alabama. Rapier said: "After all, this question resolves itself into this: either I am a man or I am not a man. If I am a man I am entitled to all privileges and immunities to which any other American citizen is entitled." [126]

Rapier was described at this time as tall, dark, with a gleam of fun in his eyes, and with an expression of internal satisfaction. He was an insatiable reader but original in his expressions. Miss LeBaron observed that he was spoken of with great respect in the House.[127]

In the summer of 1874 Rapier was renominated almost unanimously, but the carpetbaggers were not satisfied. There were rumors of secret trades of votes by which Rapier would be sacrificed. Strobach led this discontent in Montgomery. Rapier went to the White House with the carpetbaggers, Hays and Spencer, to urge President Grant to sign the Civil Rights Bill if it passed. But this gesture of party unity was not sufficient, and Rapier was defeated by J. N. Williams, the Democrat, by 1,000 majority.[128]

By 1876 the Democrats controlled the legislature and gerrymandered the congressional districts so that only one would be Republican. It was supposed that this new fourth district would be strongly Negro and Republican. But Haralson bolted when Rapier was nominated. The national and state administrations threw their support to Rapier, but Haralson was more popular with the Negroes. The result was that both were defeated by the Democrat, C. M. Shelley. Rapier was then given a position in the United States revenue service.

[126] *Ibid.*, 2nd Sess., p. 1001.

[127] *National Republican*, April 16, 1874, quoting St. Louis *Globe*.

[128] Montgomery *Journal*, August 26, 1874; Mobile *Register*, September 22, 1874; *World Almanac*, 1875.

This he held until his death, May 31, 1883, in Montgomery.[129]

The third member of the Alabama group was the best natural politician of all. Jeremiah Haralson was born near Columbus, Georgia, April 1, 1846. Moving to Alabama after the war, he became a power in politics for a decade. As early as 1868 he ran for Congress but was defeated. Then he served in the legislature, 1870-1874, where he became very popular with his race. Haralson was a pure-blooded Negro, and he capitalized on this fact whenever necessary.[130]

Haralson was strong enough by 1874 to try again for Congress. Civil rights had divided the party in the state, but he boldly stated that all must support the proposal. The white Radicals had met in Mobile to record themselves in opposition, but he obtained the floor and held them in line. The *Register's* story of his mastery is significant:

Here, black as the ace of spades and with the brogue of the cornfield, ascended the rostrum. A burly Negro, shrewd and fully aware of the strength of his people, insolent to his opponents and always advancing his line of battle while professing to desire nothing but the rights of his race, uncompromising, irritating and bold—Jere struck consternation to the scalawag soul.[131]

Here was a typical Negro politician who ran riot in the legislatures, the antithesis of the cultured Rapier and the scholarly Langston. The *Register* considered him "by far the most prominent Negro in the state" and suggested him for a vacancy in Grant's cabinet.[132]

At the district convention at Selma, Judge Busteed urged

[129] *National Republican*, September 16, 1876; Mobile *Register*, November 22, 1876; *Cong. Directory*, p. 1445.
[130] *Ibid.*, p. 1058.
[131] Mobile *Register*, June 18, 1874.
[132] *Ibid.*, June 24, 1874.

Haralson's candidacy, saying that a Negro should represent the district and the blacker the better. Haralson was nominated over another Negro and a white man. After a strenuous campaign he was elected over Bromberg, a Liberal Republican.[133]

When the House was organized in December, 1875, the members drew for seats, and Haralson received seventh choice. He modestly selected a back seat but his party associates prevailed on him to take a better one. He might have kept the distant seat, for he made no speech during either session. A few bills were introduced by him but none were passed. But he attended and voted with the party in nearly everything. During the "disputed election" session of 1876-1877 he opposed investigation of the Louisiana returning board.[134]

Bromberg contested his seat, but Haralson was sustained by this strongly Democratic House. Yet the committee found flagrant frauds and abuses on Haralson's part. Flood relief supplies had been diverted to the highlands and used to influence votes. Federal troops had also interfered in the election. However, it was clear that making these allowances Haralson was elected by a safe majority.[135]

The best service that Haralson rendered at this time was in trying to bring racial good will in Alabama. Like many others he linked universal suffrage with general amnesty and favored both. Answering criticism in Alabama, Haralson sent forth his defense in an open letter. He knew Rapier opposed him on the issue but asked: "Is it not better for us in general, especially in the South, that there be good feeling between white and black? We must drive out these hell

---

[133] *Ibid.*, August 12 and 14, 1874.

[134] *Cong. Rec.*, 43rd Cong., 1st Sess., pp. 771, 2714, 3602; 2nd Sess., pp. 132, 274, 1051, 1071.

[135] *Ibid.*, 1st Sess., pp. 1913, 2552-2553.

hounds and go in for peace between the two races in the South." [136]

This attitude did not please the regulars in Alabama, and Rapier was selected to replace him. They accused him of being too friendly toward Gordon, Lamar, and Jefferson Davis. He had also opposed the use of troops in 1876, saying: "Every blue jacket sent to the South makes Democratic votes." He received more votes than Rapier, but both were defeated.[137]

In 1878 and 1884 Haralson made the race but was easily defeated, receiving only 600 votes in 1884. He held unimportant federal appointive offices at irregular intervals. Finally he went to Colorado and was killed by wild beasts about 1916.[138]

Mississippi

Reconstruction conditions in Mississippi have already been set forth in relating the careers of Senators Revels and Bruce. The only Negro to represent Mississippi in the House had an even more interesting and varied experience in politics than did the senators.

John Roy Lynch was born September 10, 1847, near Vidalia, Louisiana. His mother was a slave, but his white father was rich and considered of high character. An arrangement had been made to free mother and son, but the father died suddenly, and a false friend failed to carry out the agreement. Instead, both were sold and taken in 1863 to Natchez, Mississippi. Here the boy attended school, studied photography and law, and was admitted to the bar. Then in 1869,

[136] Mobile *Register*, January 29, 1876.

[137] Charleston *News and Courier*, July 10, 1876; Montgomery *Journal*, October 20, 1876.

[138] New York *Times*, November 3, 1878, November 29, 1884; *Cong. Directory*, p. 1058. The author interviewed Thomas Walker, a Negro lawyer of Washington who knew Turner, Rapier, and Haralson well, and who furnished details of their careers.

when only twenty-one, Lynch began his remarkable political career. He was justice of the peace until December 31, when he resigned to serve four years in the state legislature. At the age of twenty-four Lynch was elected Speaker of the House and filled the position very creditably. Even the Democrats recognized his efficient and impartial presiding and joined the Republicans in presenting him with a gold watch and chain at the close of the 1873 session. Already in November, 1872, he had been elected to Congress from the sixth district, having a 6,000 majority over Cassidy, Democrat.[189]

When Congress convened in December, 1873, Lynch became a member of the Committee on Expenditures in the Interior Department, and of Mines and Mining. Although he was the youngest member of the Forty-third Congress, he seemed fully at ease from the first and made a formal speech within eight days. He secured the enactment of two laws in his first session, which was quite an unusual achievement.[140]

But the feature which Lynch considered his greatest contribution was his speech in advocacy of civil rights, delivered during the second session of the Forty-third Congress. The subject was almost threadbare by that time and necessarily he covered the same arguments, but his organization and logic were good. Lynch defended the constitutionality of the measure and believed that, instead of causing friction, it would allay racial strife. Nor was it a question of social equality but simply of justice. He regarded social equality as a matter between persons and not between races. He felt that he was socially superior to some white members of Congress. Even mixed schools would not be harmful, but he did not think they would be compulsory, even when so specified. He thought that the South was becoming reconciled to the new

[189] *Cong. Directory,* p. 1246; Barnes, *History of Forty-third Congress,* p. 329; Garner, *op. cit.,* p. 296, n. 1.

[140] *Cong. Rec.,* 43rd Cong., 1st Sess., pp. 74, 118, 119, 1121, 3770. Lynch was the youngest man ever elected to Congress.

order and that opposition was not half as strong as to earlier measures of this kind.[141]

Lynch's description by Miss LeBaron pictured him as looking even younger than his years. He was of a light complexion, had bright, quick, black eyes, regular features, curly, black hair, well-shaped head, aristocratic hands and feet. He was said to speak fluently, with a terseness, as if his subject matter were well weighed, and his speech contained no negroisms or provincial accent.[142]

By 1875 however, the Democrats were making a strong effort to win the state, and Lynch had a much harder fight than before. He was nominated by acclamation but his opponent, Colonel Roderick Seal, was popular in the district. Lynch made an active canvass, while Bruce and other Negro leaders attempted to rally the whole race to his support, but the official vote in November gave him only 200 majority. This, however, made him the only Republican congressman from the state.[143]

As the Democrats carried the state offices in 1875 and the electoral vote in 1876, Lynch gave much time in the Forty-fourth Congress to an attack on Democratic methods in Mississippi. In his main speech, August 12, 1876, he claimed that both elections were stolen, that affairs had been well-conducted under Governor Ames, and that the whole trouble was due to the Bourbon Democrats, who were resolved to rule or ruin. Yet Lynch expressed a desire for conciliation. He declared: "I have friends there on both sides. My home is there. My interests are there, my relatives are there, and I want to see the state happy and prosperous." [144]

Lynch was recognized as a race leader by being asked to

141 *Ibid.*, 2nd Sess., pp. 940-946.

142 *National Republican*, April 16, 1874, quoting St. Louis *Globe*.

143 Natchez *Daily Democrat and Courier*, September 23, October 2, 3, 10, 18, November 3, 30, 1875.

144 *Cong. Rec.*, 44th Cong., 1st Sess., pp. 5540-5542.

deliver a eulogy of Vice-President Wilson, who died in 1875. Lynch carried out his part in a very creditable manner and made it an occasion for a plea for removal of racial prejudice from politics.[145]

Lynch went down to defeat in the Democratic tide of 1876. General J. R. Chalmers, a man popular with both races, had opposed him. Evidently Lynch realized his defeat was legal, for although he talked of contesting it, he did not.[146] But like Smalls, Lynch was to come back to Congress later, after Reconstruction.

Louisiana

Louisiana had a slight majority of Negroes, but only one of them served in Congress; and he made practically no impression. No doubt the very corrupt politics of the Negroes reacted against them.

Charles Edmund Nash was born May 23, 1844, at Opelousas, Louisiana. During the war he enlisted as a private in the United States Volunteers and was promoted to the rank of sergeant major. He lost a leg at Fort Blakely and was then honorably discharged. Nash did not have the political experience which most Negroes had before they were elected to Congress. It is hard to understand how his election was brought about, as he did not hold a dominant position in the party. Probably the party leaders expected to use him for their purposes.[147]

He was elected to the Forty-fourth Congress, which was Democratic. Yet he was admitted without a contest and was appointed on the Committee on Education and Labor. He proposed several local bills but spoke in advocacy of none, and none of them passed.[148]

[145] *Ibid.*, pp. 546, 547.
[146] Jackson *Clarion*, January 31, 1877; *National Republican*, December 7, 1876.
[147] *Cong. Directory*, p. 1349.
[148] *Cong. Rec.*, 44th Cong., 1st Sess., pp. 251, 305.

The only speech which Nash made in either session was on the stock subject of his black colleagues—the political condition of the South. However, to do him justice, his only speech was an excellent one, and breathed in general a spirit of reconciliation. To be sure the only hope of the South was to become Republican, and it sounded strange to hear his defense of Longstreet and other Confederates who had become scalawags. Yet Nash held that the war bitterness was fast passing. In fine spirit he said: "We are not enemies but brethren.... This country is our joint inheritance.... Over brothers' graves let brothers' quarrels die. Let there be peace between us that these swords which we have learned to use so well, may if used again, strike only at a common foe." [149]

In the eventful campaign of 1876, Nash played only a minor part. He did not rank at all with Pinchback, Packard, and Kellogg within the state. Defeated for delegate-at-large to the National Convention, he was elected only as a district delegate. He was renominated in the sixth district but his own party organ was not enthusiastic in his support. He was not active in canvassing the state, though many speakers were pressed into service. Packard had a crowd of 4,000 at Nash's home town, and yet Nash's name was not mentioned. It is not surprising that due to these factors the largest shift in the state occurred in his district. Robertson, the Democrat, had over 5,000 majority. This defeat ended Nash's political career, and he withdrew into obscurity until his death in New Orleans June 21, 1913.[150]

[149] *Ibid.*, pp. 3667-3669.
[150] New Orleans *Times,* June to November, 1876; New Orleans *Republican,* June to November, 1876; *Cong. Directory,* p. 1349.

IV

THE NEGRO IN THE HOUSE OF REPRESENT-
ATIVES AFTER RECONSTRUCTION,
1877-1901

No SOONER was Reconstruction accomplished, than attempts at its undoing were started. The whites in the South were reconciled to their military defeat but they never accepted Negro political control as a permanent fact. As the Negroes were inseparably wedded to the Republican party and, in nearly all of the South, formed its major element, the Republican party must be defeated by fair means or foul. The party name of "Democrat" was often replaced by "Conservative," in order to appeal to former Southern Whigs, and to Northern whites who had come South. Success rewarded this effort, although it seemed long delayed in some states. Home rule was won in Tennessee in 1869, in Virginia in 1869-1870, and in North Carolina and Georgia in 1870. There was little gain in the period 1870-1874 but the victories won were being consolidated. In 1874 Alabama, Arkansas, and Texas passed under white control, and in 1875 Mississippi was added. Final victory came in 1876-1877 when Florida, South Carolina, and Louisiana regained home rule, with the tacit consent of the Hayes administration.[1]

Within these states, however, in many sections Negroes still controlled county and local offices. But now the whites had the great advantage of the state machinery and used it

[1] Walter L. Fleming, *The Sequel of Appomattox,* Chronicles of America Series, XXXII, 290-302.

to the fullest extent. Some regions were put under executive control and were ruled by commission. Yet in spite of all these precautions, ten Negroes served in Congress during the undoing of the Reconstruction.[2]

SOUTH CAROLINA

In 1876 the whites in South Carolina had stemmed the black tide, but they were not able to drive it back completely. The state ticket had been elected by very narrow margins, but three Negroes had been re-elected to Congress, Rainey and Smalls being continued in office, and Cain being returned after the lapse of one term. The *News and Courier* had been slow to adopt a "straight out" policy in 1876 but was now fully committed to it, and denounced all three men as unfit. The charges against Rainey were vague, while the other two were accused outright of overt crimes. It was predicted that this was Rainey's last term in Congress unless Connecticut sent him—he had a costly residence near Windsor, Connecticut.[3]

J. S. Richardson contested Rainey's seat, but on the second day of the session Rainey was seated. In South Carolina the decision was considered an outrage. Northern Democrats were accused of being timid when the claimants were Negroes, and even Southern Democrats were accused of seeking credit for liberalism by favoring them.[4]

Although he was admitted so easily, Rainey nevertheless seemed awed by the Democratic House, for he introduced no measures and spoke only in regard to his certificate of election from the board of state canvassers.[5]

[2] *Ibid.*, p. 303.
[3] Charleston *News and Courier*, October 9, 1877.
[4] *Ibid.*, October 22, 1877.
[5] *Cong. Rec.*, 45th Cong., 1st Sess., pp. 62-63.

In his next and final session he was almost as inarticulate. His only speech on the floor was a eulogy of J. E. Leonard, a Louisiana carpetbagger, and he obtained leave to print a defense of the Freedmen's Bank management. Rainey claimed that the failure was due not to fraud but to natural business shrinkage. However, a great majority of both races differed with him.[6]

Rainey campaigned for the party in Michigan during the summer of 1878, and then returned to South Carolina in August to help Smalls, but he made only a halfhearted canvass in his own district. Evidently he felt that his race was a forlorn hope this time, and so it was. The tables were at last turned, and Rainey was defeated by a majority of more than 8,000 votes.[7]

As his final session drew to a close in March, 1879, there were conflicting estimates of the value of his services in Congress. To be sure, he had served eight and a half years, a record up to the present for his race. But during that long period, had he done anything really useful? The *Republican* thought that he could have been governor in 1874 had he expressed a desire, that his good name had never been detracted from, and that he would "yet be elevated to a position commensurate with his sterling worth when law and the Constitution are again respected in South Carolina." But the *News and Courier* replied that his reputation was good because he left the state before stealing was general, and if he had done "an earthly thing to benefit the state or his constituents nobody has ever heard of it. Of course he makes friends (Fernando Wood calls him a good fellow) as he did when he followed his first trade of barber, by putting a smooth face on it." The substance of this was that he had been a harm-

---

[6] *Ibid.*, 2nd Sess., p. 332, Appendix, p. 98.
[7] *National Republican*, August 17, 1878; Charleston *News and Courier*, November 15 and December 13, 1878.

less, negative member; not a corruptionist but not one who obtained results.[8]

The Forty-sixth Congress was called in special session in March, 1879. It was a Democratic House but Rainey was the unanimous complimentary choice of the Republicans for Clerk of the House. Contenting himself with an internal revenue clerkship for two years, he resigned in 1881, for the Republicans had recaptured the House and surely now, he thought, they would redeem their promises to him. Taking a room at the Willard, the finest hotel in Washington, he began an active campaign. Every Republican whom he approached encouraged him, but at the caucus McPherson received the nomination by a majority of fifty. Rainey swallowed his pride and said he hoped to receive a place under McPherson, but he did not. As the Negroes could no longer deliver electoral votes in the South, the Republicans saw no reason for catering to them. Rainey soon returned to his old home in South Carolina, thus ending the career of the Negro who served longest in Congress. He died there on August 2, 1887.[9]

The seat of Cain was contested when Congress met, but he was admitted by a large vote by this Democratic House. Emboldened by his success, his principal speech of the session was a defense of the use of federal troops in South Carolina in 1876. Cain claimed that the emergency justified their use and that even in 1878 the army should not be reduced. He introduced a number of bills, principally of a private and local nature.[10] One, of a broader nature, proposed to apply the surplus of public lands, lapsed from railroads, to public education. This gave him an opportunity to stress the value of education. His arguments were sound until he made a

[8] Charleston *News and Courier*, March 1, 1879, quoting *National Republican*.
[9] Philadelphia *Inquirer*, March 18, 1879; *National Republican*, December 2-5, 1881; *Cong. Directory*, p. 1440.
[10] *Cong. Rec.*, 45th Cong., 1st Sess., pp. 65, 722; 2nd Sess., pp. 1646, 3683.

panacea of education. In education he saw the cure for intemperance, crime, and racial antagonism.[11]

The *News and Courier* was infuriated by his attempt to prove more illiteracy among whites than among blacks, and it commented:

The arithmetic of Congressman Cain is as lax as his morality.... Congressman Cain, true to his nature, was more anxious to astonish and amuse his audience than to get at the facts. It is a misfortune that the colored people should recognize bellowing rogues of his class as their leaders.[12]

It had been Cain's misfortune to lose favor at home, even with his own race. When the second district convention met in 1878 he was abused and deposed unanimously for E. W. M. Mackey, a scalawag. Strange to say, the Negroes accused Cain of being too friendly with the whites.[13]

In 1880 he was elected a bishop of his church and was assigned to Louisiana and Texas. For a time he was also president of Paul Quinn College, Waco, Texas. Returning to Washington, he died there January 18, 1887.[14]

As Elliott lost prestige in 1876, he was succeeded in party influence not by the cautious Rainey nor by the professed reformer, Cain, but by the aggressive and frank partisan, Smalls. His county of Beaufort had a larger percentage of Negroes than any other county in the United States; Smalls was the idol of these Negroes and Beaufort County had a strong influence on the rest of the district, which was black also. In case they did not vote for him, he took care that they were counted for him. Consequently in 1876, he was reelected by 1,500 majority. Tillman filled 694 pages of evi-

[11] *Ibid.*, 3rd Sess., pp. 683-688.
[12] Charleston *News and Courier*, February 3, 1879.
[13] *Ibid.*, October 26, 1878.
[14] *Dictionary of American Biography*, III, 404; Washington *Post*, January 19, 1887.

dence that he (Tillman) was entitled to the seat, but the Democratic House denied his claim.[15]

Another contest, however, caused Smalls trouble during all this session. The Democratic legislature made a thorough investigation of the Reconstruction legislatures and it was disclosed that Smalls had accepted a bribe of $5,000 to favor the Republican Printing Company. He was indicted, arrested and convicted, and sentenced to three years' hard labor. He appealed, but the South Carolina Supreme Court affirmed the sentence. Then the Democratic Governor, Simpson, pardoned him on condition that Smalls throw himself on the mercy of the court, and abandon his motion for transfer to United States court. Smalls always maintained that this was political persecution, and that he had not asked for pardon. No doubt there was political bias in his prosecution. Nevertheless, the bank check that he received was produced, and the jury was composed of seven Negroes and five whites.[16]

Meeting these attacks consumed much of Smalls's time, and he took little part in the deliberations of the Forty-fifth Congress. He did some worth-while work, however, in trying to recover damages suffered by his district due to its long occupation during the war. But a Democratic House feared to be too kindly to the devastated districts for fear the North would resent such action.[17]

When Smalls returned to his district in 1878, he received an ovation and was renominated. It is hard to determine how his fortunes had been affected by his conviction for bribery. The *News and Courier* remarked that he seemed to possess the confidence of his race to a degree that no other Negro could hope to attain. "The men, women, and children seem to regard him with a feeling akin to worship." Smalls was de-

[15] Charleston *News and Courier*, December 11, 1877.

[16] *Tribune Almanac*, 1877; Charleston *News and Courier*, October 10, November 12, 1877; November 15, 1878; September 9, October 21, 1878.

[17] *Cong. Rec.*, 45th Cong., 2nd Sess., pp. 1457, 2706; 3rd Sess., p. 1446.

feated by Tillman, but this was caused more by aggression of the whites than by defection of the blacks. The famous red-shirts of 1876 were again active except where the Negroes were in a hopeless majority. St. Helena Island had 910 Negro voters and 909 of them voted for Smalls, but in other sections the Democrats secured better results and defeated him.[18]

At this time Sir George Campbell, member of Parliament, was on a visit to Beaufort and was very favorably impressed by Smalls. He said that Smalls had great influence among his race and was well liked by the whites. Later Sir George said, "I still like General Smalls on further acquaintance. He is not very highly educated nor brilliant but is a thoroughly representative man among the people and seems to have their unlimited confidence." [19]

By 1880 Smalls had regained confidence and decided to make the race again. There was some opposition to him within the party, due to his past record. The district chairman resigned and denounced Smalls as unfit, while several prominent Republicans in Beaufort bolted him. Undismayed, Smalls made a vigorous campaign and declared he was innocent of the charges. The official returns showed Tillman over 8,000 votes ahead, but the Republican House of the Forty-seventh Congress reversed this large popular majority and seated Smalls, July 19, 1882.[20]

Smalls may have been entitled to the seat, but, believing it to be a partisan decision, all the Democrats filibustered and finally refused to vote. To be sure, fallacious arguments were used here as in a number of other contests when Negroes were

---

[18] R. S. Holland, *Letters and Diary of Laura M. Towne*, pp. 289, 292. Miss Towne was a New England missionary to Beaufort. She adored Smalls and often entertained him on terms of social equality. See also *National Republican*, July 22, 1878, quoting *News and Courier*.

[19] A. A. Taylor, *The Negro in South Carolina During the Reconstruction*, p. 158. Quoted by permission of The Associated Publishers, Inc.

[20] Charleston *News and Courier*, September 4 and 6, and October 4 and 21, 1880; *Cong. Rec.*, 47th Cong., 1st Sess., p. 6234.

involved. It was assumed that Negroes always voted Republican and that all of them voted. As a matter of fact, by 1880 many of them had lost interest or had personal reasons for opposing a man of Smalls's record. So it was clearly unjust to assume that the Republican vote was small because of suppression.[21]

The first session was almost ended when he was seated. But in the next session he secured an appropriation for Port Royal storehouse and docks. An attempt to put Smalls on the navy retired list as a captain failed, as did a related bill proposing a large grant to Smalls for his capture of the Confederate ship, "Planter," in 1863.[22]

The state legislature had gerrymandered the congressional districts so as to make the seventh a black, Republican district but all the others Democratic. This practically made Republican nomination equivalent to election if any considerable number of Negroes voted. Smalls sought to capitalize this by demanding a Negro candidate for this new district. But Samuel Lee, another Negro, and E. W. M. Mackey, a scalawag, opposed him. After a bitter convention lasting a week, Smalls for the sake of harmony came to Mackey's aid. Mackey was nominated. The Democrats made no nomination, but Lee ran independently. Mackey, however, was popular with the Negroes and had married a woman who had Negro blood. Consequently, he was elected over Lee.[23]

Mackey died January 28, 1884, and Smalls was elected without opposition to fill the vacancy.[24] Again he failed to secure a refund of direct taxes levied on Beaufort during the war and to get an adequate appropriation for Charleston harbor.[25]

21 *Ibid.*, pp. 6213, 6218-6219.
22 *Ibid.*, 2nd Sess., pp. 3196, 3437-3440, 307.
23 Charleston *News and Courier*, September 23 and 30, and November 9, 1882.
24 *Tribune Almanac*, 1885.
25 *Cong. Rec.*, 48th Cong., 1st Sess., p. 5202; 2nd Sess., p. 1396.

Smalls's principal support in this Forty-eighth Congress was given to an interstate commerce bill providing equal accommodations for the races. The Crisp amendment proposed equal but separate accommodations. Smalls opposed the amendment and yet admitted that in South Carolina there was no discrimination.[26]

In the autumn of 1884, Smalls won his last victory. He used all the arts of a politician and proved himself an expert in the political game. Wherever the whites were present in numbers he was conciliatory, but in other places he harangued the Negroes. As his Democratic opponent, Elliott, was a Confederate veteran, Smalls stressed the fact that he himself had fought in Federal service. He also drew the color line and told the Negroes to spend the day around the polls whether they had registration certificates or not. The notorious Negro corruptionist, Whipper, campaigned for Smalls and resorted to his usual demagoguery. He threatened that if Elliott were elected "we will raise hell with the whites down here." The Negroes responded to these appeals, and Smalls received 4,000 majority.[27] A month later Hampton was reelected to the Senate, while Smalls was receiving for the Senate three complimentary votes in the leigislature.[28] His influence, strong in his own district, was not state-wide.

Probably realizing that this would be his last chance, Smalls did his best work in the Forty-ninth Congress. He had not attained facility in serious, sustained speech, but was still more successful in short, pointed support of some object he favored or in opposition to the Democratic majority. Smalls was a familiar figure in Congress because of his long service. He was short and had become very stout, but with his white whiskers

---

[26] *Ibid.*, 2nd Sess., p. 316.

[27] Charleston *News and Courier*, October 22 and 25, and November 3 and 28, 1884.

[28] *Ibid.*, December 10, 1884.

he made a good appearance. In spite of his early deficiency in education, he had trained himself and could talk correctly and write a good letter. Down in the black district, however, he spoke in Gullah dialect.[29]

As a member of the War Claims Committee he submitted fifteen war claims, while, on his own initiative, he presented eight private claims, introduced thirteen private bills and seven public ones, and proposed amendments to two pending bills—all in the first session. It is interesting to note that one of his relief bills was in behalf of John C. Frémont. Nearly all of his legislative attempts failed, but it was most unusual for a Negro member to even attempt so much. He, however, succeeded with three private relief bills, and with an amendment to the Naval Appropriation Bill.[30]

Two prepared speeches of his could not be delivered because of the press of time, but he was given leave to print. One of these is interesting, for it throws light on Smalls's career. President Cleveland had vetoed a pension for the widow of General Hunter. In favoring an overriding of the veto, Smalls revealed his close relations to Hunter, Stanton, and Lincoln. The authorization for the formation of Negro regiments was contained in a letter given Smalls by Lincoln. However, the veto was upheld.[31]

In the next session, his Negro colleague, O'Hara of North Carolina, introduced a bill for the relief of Smalls and his crew of the famous "Planter." The bill went to committee and died there. However, this appeared to be a perennial bill, for Joseph Cannon introduced it again in the Fiftieth Congress. The bill would have given Smalls about $30,000; it was felt, however, that he had been paid enough already, and the bill

[29] The author interviewed Dr. C. G. Woodson and Clerk of the House, W. T. Page, November, 1929. Clerk Page was a page at the time Smalls was in Congress and had a clear recollection of him.

[30] *Cong. Rec.*, 49th Cong., 1st Sess., *passim*, especially p. 3401.

[31] *Ibid.*, p. 7746, Appendix, pp. 319, 330.

was blocked by Samuel Dibble, a South Carolina Democrat.[32] This ended the famous "Planter" episode as far as Congress was concerned.

An analysis of the yeas and nays during Smalls's tenure showed what a thorough partisan he was. Cleveland was trying to pension only those who were deserving and not to use pensions for political purposes. Smalls always voted for general pensions and for overriding the veto of private pensions. He supported the spoilsmen in their opposition to civil service reform and opposed repeal of the Tenure of Office Act.[33]

The shrewd campaigner made his last race in 1886. The national and state administrations combined to defeat him. Senator Hampton brought word that President Cleveland was personally interested, and Dibble, in charge of the Democratic Congressional Committee, gave special attention to the seventh district. On the other hand the local Republicans were torn by dissension. There had arisen a peculiar color line of blacks against yellows and neutral tints. The pure blacks turned away from Smalls, as they said he had favored his own lighter shades. As a result of all these things, Elliott defeated him by a safe vote. The New York *Enterprise*, a leading Negro paper, accepted his defeat calmly and said:

There is not a single instance in his political history as a member of Congress where he has ever put forth a measure to promote the interests of his race. . . . He was more of a target of ridicule than a statesman. . . . He has only retained his place so long because though ignorant himself, he was just smart enough to gain the support and confidence of the black voters in his district by his outward seeming and flattery.[34]

[32] *Ibid.*, 49th Cong., 2nd Sess., pp. 289, 670; Charleston *News and Courier*, July 31, 1888.

[33] *Cong. Rec.*, 47th Cong., 1st Sess., pp. 867, 1165; 49th Cong., 1st Sess., pp. 2226, 2675, 2696, 2700.

[34] Charleston *News and Courier*, October 16 and 18, and November 9, 1886. (Quotes New York *Enterprise* in November 9 issue.)

Lodge sponsored his contest in the Fiftieth Congress, and Smalls was allowed to speak in his own behalf, but he was not admitted.[85]

In 1888 he was at last persuaded to retire in favor of T. E. Miller, a younger Negro. Smalls was sent to the national convention, and when the other delegates deserted Sherman, Smalls continued loyal. As a reward Sherman influenced President Harrison to appoint Smalls collector of the port of Beaufort. He retired in 1913 and died February 22, 1915.[86]

Before Smalls's death the bitterness of Reconstruction had faded out, and the whites of Beaufort speak well of him. They feel that Smalls did not stir up the trouble but only took advantage of it. The very kind treatment which he showed his former old mistress, who was in need, impressed the whites very much. The discord within the Negro race had subsided, and Miller, a rival who displaced him, admitted that Smalls was "the greatest politician of anyone of us." [87]

The man who regained the district which Smalls had lost was a native of the same county but a younger man, who had grown up since the war. Thomas Ezekiel Miller was born at Ferebeeville, South Carolina, June 17, 1849. He belonged to a free Negro family which had owned slaves before the war. Miller, himself, is accounted an octoroon; yet he could be very bitter toward the whites. He attended school in Charleston, South Carolina, and Hudson, New York, and graduated from Lincoln University in 1872. He was admitted to the bar in 1875 and practiced law at Beaufort. As soon as he returned to South Carolina he entered politics, serving as county school

[85] *Cong. Rec.*, 50th Cong., 2nd Sess., pp. 255, 1878.

[86] Charleston *News and Courier*, August 27, 1888; *Cong. Directory*, p. 1553; letter from Commander Allen Stuart, U. S. N. (retired), to the author, January 14, 1930.

[87] *Ibid.*; letter from N. L. Willett to the author, January 11, 1930; letter from Thomas E. Miller to the author, March 4, 1930.

commissioner, state representative, and state senator. Within the Republican party, also, he understudied Smalls and succeeded him just as Smalls had succeeded Elliott.[88]

By 1878 Miller was prominent enough in state politics to denounce in the convention the Hampton administration. The only Republicans elected to the legislature that year were from Beaufort County, and Miller was one of them. The *News and Courier* thought he was better fitted for jail. The Springfield *Republican* considered it discreditable to the party to have a candidate like Miller and said that he should not be counted out but should be tried in the courts. Hampton was elected to the United States Senate by this legislature, but Miller and his colleague had the empty satisfaction of voting for Mackey, a scalawag. It was said that "a thrill of disgust ran through the assembly." [39]

In the state convention of 1880 a slate of state offices was proposed with Miller on it for lieutenant-governor, but Elliott persuaded the party to make no state fight that year, but to concentrate instead on the electoral ticket.[40]

When Smalls was in temporary disfavor in 1882, Miller supported Mackey, the nominee of the year, instead of the bolter, Lee. As a reward for his regularity, by the next campaign year Miller had become state chairman. He harangued the convention, stressed the color line, and urged the Negroes to put out local and state tickets if they had to take up collections in their churches to pay expenses. But the *News and Courier* thought that "Tom is not as bitter as his speeches indicate. He is speaking for effect." [41] It was true that Miller

---

[88] *Cong. Directory*, p. 1315; Charleston *News and Courier*, October 25, 1886; letter from Commander Allen Stuart to the author, January 14, 1930; letter from N. L. Willett to the author, January 11, 1930.

[39] Charleston *News and Courier*, November 19 and 25, and December 11, 1878. The issue of November 25, 1878, quoted the Springfield *Republican*.

[40] Charleston *News and Courier*, September 3 and 4, 1880.

[41] *Ibid.*, September 28, 1882; April 16 and 17, 1884.

could suit his speech to the times and the audience. This was shown in 1886 when he deplored the color line within the color line, and said he was sorry that he was light colored but he could not help it.[42]

As a result of his political experience Miller won the nomination on the first ballot in 1888. Both parties made great efforts to win this election. Miller went to Washington and enlisted the support of Quay, Sherman, and others. On the other hand, all whites were urged to vote early and often, at least nine times, as there were seven state boxes and two federal ones. The whites responded so well that they gave Elliott over 1,330 majority.[43]

The Republicans controlled the House in the Fifty-first Congress but by a very narrow margin, and they seized every chance to increase their strength. It was at this time that Speaker Reed inaugurated the new practice of counting a member present if he were present but had not answered the roll call. After a bitter contest Langston, a Virginia Negro, was seated while the Democrats were all absent as a protest. Then at once, with the Democrats still absent, Miller's contest was taken up; no debate was allowed, and he was seated by a vote of 157 to 1. This was clearly a partisan procedure as Elliott, the incumbent, was not given a chance to defend himself. It was done to hold in line the Negro vote, which was wavering. In some cases, however, white Republicans were defeated because Congress had been held in session so long that these members had only a month to campaign for re-election.[44]

[42] *Ibid.*, October 25, 1886.

[43] Charleston *News and Courier*, September 12, October 2, and November 6 and 23, 1888. The injunction in the *News and Courier* in regard to voting often has been quoted to prove encouragement of fraud. But it is obvious that the editor had no such idea.

[44] *Cong. Rec.*, 51st Cong., 1st Sess., pp. 10, 339, 379; Washington *Post*, September 23, 1890, quoting Indianapolis *Journal*. Congress had prolonged its session three weeks mainly because of this bitter partisan clash.

Miller had only a week to serve in this first session but he was not abashed by his newness. Flattered by membership on the Library of Congress Committee, he introduced bills, proposing two most chimerical schemes: one to appropriate $1,000,000 for a home for ex-slaves, the other to spend $250,-000 for a monument to the Negro soldiers killed in the war. These made good publicity but, needless to say, had no chance of passage.[45]

In the next session Miller distinguished himself in the House by his bitter tirade against the South in general, and South Carolina in particular. The bills under discussion were those for naval and Indian appropriations, but that mattered not to Miller. He urged the passage of the Force Bill and called Republicans who opposed it "a veritable set of fools." No fiercer denunciation has been delivered on the floor than his indictment of the whole South:

There is no people in the world more self-opinionated without cause, more bigoted without achievements, more boastful without a status, no people in the world so quick to misjudge their countrymen and to misstate historical facts of political economy and to impugn the motives of others. History does not record a civilized people who have been contented with so little and who can feed so long on a worthless, buried past. While crying for mercy and attempting to speak as ambassadors of peace, there are no people in the world more vituperative than her leaders.[46]

On the other hand Miller attempted to free the Negro from all blame for racial strife. He claimed that Negroes were never guilty of rape but that after a suspect was lynched, "invariably letters or verbal admissions absolve the innocent dead man from the crime charged." In fact, he said, "The Negro

[45] *Cong. Rec.*, 51st Cong., 1st Sess., pp. 10,707, 10,708.
[46] *Ibid.*, 2nd Sess., pp. 2691-2696. The daily papers of the time are full of harrowing cases of rape and lynchings, but the Negroes involved often confessed and boasted of their achievement.

is the equal of the poor, illiterate white citizen, in every element that constitutes an American, Christian citizen. And in devotion to the national government ... history records him as the superior of his white master, never a nullifier, never a carping hypocrite with foul treason in his heart." [47] Even if true, this vindictive harangue could produce no possible good.

No time was left to Miller for the support of anything nonpartisan. In his exasperation at everything Southern, he voted against refund of the cotton tax. Other Negro congressmen had accomplished little that was constructive, but had not been so antagonistic to the states they were supposed to represent.[48]

In 1890 Miller was the nominee, though E. M. Brayton, a white Republican, also ran. The organization supported Miller, and on the face of the returns he defeated Brayton and Elliott, the Democrat. But all of Miller's ballots were illegal because they were not the legal size or color. Consequently, the South Carolina Supreme Court declared Elliott was elected. Miller protested but did not carry his contest to the Fifty-second Congress.[49]

Settling in South Carolina, he served again in the legislature and in the Constitutional Convention of 1895. He made a long and eloquent protest against the "understanding" clause of the new constitution. One of his Negro eulogists ranks this oration with those of Webster and Wendell Phillips—clearly an extravagant estimate. The state government was magnanimous enough not to hold a grudge against Miller and appointed him president of the State Negro College at Orangeburg. After doing good work from 1896 to 1911, he resigned and retired to Philadelphia, but spent his winters in

---

[47] *Ibid.*
[48] *Ibid.*, p. 3225.
[49] Charleston *News and Courier*, August 15, September 19, November 12, December 30, 1890.

Charleston. The passage of time mellowed his partisanship, and strange as it seems, he is reported to have supported Smith strongly in 1928 for the presidency.[50] But the whites of Beaufort do not have the kindly feeling toward him that they had toward Smalls, although Georgetown, in his district, has relented somewhat. He died in retirement at Charleston, April 8, 1938.[51]

The last Negro who represented South Carolina in Congress was almost as old as Miller but went into politics much later. George Washington Murray was born at Rembert, Sumter County, South Carolina, September 22, 1853. He was a slave boy and had no white blood at all. At emancipation he was left a helpless orphan, and had a hard struggle for mere existence. But he managed to pick up enough education to teach. Then in 1874 he entered South Carolina University, staying until 1876, when the whites excluded all Negroes. From 1876 to 1890 he continued teaching with incidental participation in politics. In 1888 he was party chairman of Sumter County and was active in county and district campaigns that year. Probably as a reward, President Harrison made him inspector of customs at the port of Charleston.[52]

Murray had become a party leader of state renown by 1890 and was a candidate for the congressional nomination, but Miller was again chosen, and Murray remained loyal to him. He was permanent chairman of the state convention and urged a vigorous fight all along the line.[53] There was a bitter

[50] Ferris, *op. cit.*, II, 793; New York *Times*, November 4, 1895; Lester A. Walton, "The Negro Comes Back to the United States Congress," *Current History*, XXX (June, 1929), 461-463; letter to the author, March 4, 1930, from Thomas E. Miller.

[51] Letters to the author from Commander Stuart, January 14, 1930; from N. L. Willett, January 11, 1930; from Ethel Bellune, March 23, 1930; from Emma Pregnall, Chief Clerk, Charleston Health Department, November 20, 1939.

[52] *Cong. Directory*, p. 1347; D. W. Culp, *Twentieth Century Negro Literature*, p. 231; Charleston *News and Courier*, October 1, 1888.

[53] *Ibid.*, August 2 and September 19, 1890.

contest for the nomination in 1892 with Smalls, Miller, Murray, and Brayton, all in the race. But Murray was the logical candidate as he had never been defeated, and all the others had. He won on the fourth ballot and announced he would make a vigorous canvass. There was national interest in the contest, for the black district was well known. Early returns indicated Murray had lost to General Moise but Miller carried Murray's claims before the state board of canvassers and secured a certificate of election by forty majority. The amazing charge was made that the Tillmanites in control had deliberately "knifed" Moise and then counted him out because he was a Cleveland Democrat.[54]

Within less than three weeks after Congress convened, Murray made an able speech in favor of free silver. Murray was the only Negro in this, the Fifty-third Congress, and claimed that the 8,000,000 whom he represented were all in favor of free silver: "The Negro is always found voting and shooting for America and Americans and on this currency question he is in favor of an American instead of an English, German, French, or Belgian policy." He also opposed repeal of federal election laws, claiming that even under the protection of those laws 140,000 Negroes were disqualified in South Carolina, and 1,200,000 in all the South.[55]

In the next session Murray was absent most of the time because of important business or sickness. When present he advocated industrial education for the Negro. Hampton and Tuskegee were doing good work but more similar schools were needed. He also urged federal aid for the Atlanta Cotton Exposition. He felt this would create good will between the races in the South. Murray asked for the printing of a list of

[54] *Ibid.*, September 2 and 3, and November 9 and 27, 1892. After thirty-eight years this was still an issue in South Carolina politics—Columbia *State*, August 3, 1930.

[55] *Cong. Rec.*, 53rd Cong., 1st Sess., pp. 858-862, 2147-2150, 2158-2161.

ninety-two inventions, patented by Negroes. He modestly failed to mention that eight of them were his own, all for agricultural implements.[56]

During the final session of this Congress, the records do not show that he was ever present. February 1, 1895, he was given indefinite leave of absence on account of important business. Evidently his private business continued more important than public, and he did not return.[57] It is not clear, but he was probably working up his contest for the next Congress.

The legislature had redistricted the state in 1893, creating a new black district, the first district. A wail of despair went up from Charleston as the city was transferred to the black district. It seemed that she was being punished, but it was hoped that the large white vote in the city would sway the whole district. Ugly stories of a Tillman alliance with the Negroes were again circulating. The official count, however, gave Elliott more than 1,700 majority over Murray.[58]

In the Fifty-fourth Congress, the House was strongly Republican, and, therefore, pressure was brought to bear by Negroes to obtain a representative of their race. The campaign of 1896 was already opening when, just before Congress adjourned, it changed 2,000 votes in the first district of South Carolina and seated Murray.[59]

Murray was absent during much of the next session. When present, his principal activity was to present petitions from South Carolina Negroes, and to agitate for federal interference in the state elections. The Tillmanites had turned against them, to their disappointment.[60]

The final disintegration of Republicanism in South Caro-

---

[56] *Ibid.*, 2nd Sess., pp. 6177-6178, 8382.

[57] *Ibid.*, 3rd Sess., p. 1652.

[58] Charleston *News and Courier*, September 5, October 27, November 2 and 20, 1894.

[59] *Cong. Rec.*, 54th Cong., 1st Sess., pp. 6076, 6110, Appendix, p. 452.

[60] *Ibid.*, 2nd Sess., 1079, 1667, 1868.

lina came about in 1896. There was a lily-white state convention and a black-and-tan one. For some strange reason Murray met with the lily-whites. This faction controlled the district convention and nominated Cohen, a white. As the Negroes were dissatisfied, Murray led them in a bolt. Because of this division, Elliott's majority was so large that it was not disputed.[61]

Because of his bolt Murray lost the usual solace of a federal clerkship. Real estate attracted him to Sumter, but he was convicted of fraud and fled to Chicago while under bond. There he engaged in literary work and lecturing, dying there April 21, 1926.[62]

MISSISSIPPI

John R. Lynch was more powerful within his state than any of the South Carolina group within that state. There was only one black district in Mississippi, and Lynch always had the nomination if he wished it. There were other influential Negroes in Mississippi but they were satisfied with other honors. Lynch let the district go by default in 1878 but he resolved to try again in 1880. The *Clarion* admitted Lynch's strength: "The Republicans of the sixth district have nominated Lynch. He was formerly a member and is the ablest man of his race in the South." Chalmers made a thorough canvass for the Democrats and apparently had over 3,000 majority. He explained that more Negroes had supported him than ever, but Lynch declared Chalmers' large vote was due to fraud, and filed notice of a contest.[63]

When the Forty-seventh Congress convened, his contest was filed but it was April, 1882, before it came up for a decision. The committee had reported in favor of Lynch, and

[61] Charleston *News and Courier*, September 16 and 18, and November 24, 1896.
[62] *Cong. Directory*, p. 1347; letter from Esther Osteen to the author, March 15, 1930, relative to real estate affair.
[63] Jackson *Clarion*, July 14, October 20, November 18, and December 2, 1880.

he was invited to present his case. This he did very ably and extensively. In this, Lynch contended that Chalmers had controlled all the machinery of election and had practically dictated the result. Yet he insisted that the trouble was not due to race prejudice at all, but only to partisanship. Lynch hoped that this would soon pass away and to this end he invoked "the considerate judgment of mankind and the gracious favor of Almighty God." Chalmers claimed that Lynch was unpopular because he had opposed Grant for a third term in 1880. The House chose to accept Lynch's statement and seated him.[64]

This session soon adjourned, but in the next session Lynch made several set addresses. These showed that he was interested especially in education, wished federal aid for it, and thought it only fair for the wealthy North to help the devastated South. He also favored a protective tariff on cotton, lumber, and sugar, thinking a tariff would build up these products.[65]

In his request for reasonable appropriations for Southern rivers and harbors, Lynch made the interesting comment that the South would not support a party that did not support the South. He was sure many Southern whites had voted for him, as he had reversed a Democratic majority.[66]

Lynch always voted with the administration and so, in this last Congress in which he served, he supported the administration tariff and pension bill and voted to unseat J. S. Richardson on the last day of the session.[67]

In 1882 he was defeated by only 600 but in 1884 he lost by 4,600 and he then gave up all hope of ever regaining the dis-

---

[64] *Cong. Rec.*, 47th Cong., 1st Sess., pp. 244, 3384-3390, 3451. In a letter to the author December 14, 1928, Lynch said he considered this one of the best speeches of his career.

[65] *Ibid.*, 2nd Sess., pp. 1205, 2312, 2660, 2870.

[66] *Ibid.*, p. 158.

[67] *Ibid.*, pp. 1165, 3742, 3752.

trict. But Lynch received many honors after that, and probably less than any other Negro congressman is his fame dependent on his congressional career.[68]

In 1884 he received an honor which no other Negro has yet enjoyed. Through efforts of Roosevelt, Lodge, Wadsworth, White, and Fish he was elected temporary chairman of the Republican national convention and presided part of two days with general satisfaction. He even received nine out of thirty-seven committee votes for permanent chairman. Other Negroes have been called to the chair for a few minutes but Lynch's honor was quite distinctive.[69]

Cleveland was elected in 1884; Lynch was offered a federal position under him then, and again in Cleveland's second term, but declined both times. Under Harrison he served, 1889-1893, as an auditor of the Treasury for the Navy Department. In 1896 he was admitted to the bar and practiced. But in 1898 he entered the army, serving until 1911 when he was retired with the rank of major. When well over eighty years of age he maintained a law office in Chicago and at times wrote on Reconstruction. He also engaged in writing "Reminiscences of an Active Life," which should be well worth while for students of the Reconstruction years. However, this has not yet been published. He died in Chicago, November 2, 1939.[70] He was the last congressional member of either race who had been prominent in Reconstruction days.

Blaine singles out Rainey, Rapier, and Lynch for special mention of Negro congressmen. Rhodes says Lynch was a credit to his race. So, as far as Rhodes is concerned, his reputation seems secure. Incidentally, Rhodes was rather severe in

---

[68] *Ibid.*, Appendix, p. 158; Jackson *Clarion*, November 12, 1884.

[69] New York *Sun*, June 4-9, 1884.

[70] *Cong. Directory*, p. 1246; letter from J. R. Lynch to the author, December 14, 1928; Lynch, *op. cit.*, pp. 235-239, 277-281. Lynch declined holding office under Cleveland for fear it would injure his party leadership.—Letter from J. R. Lynch to the author, July 21, 1939. New York *Times*, November 3, 1939.

his judgments on Reconstruction in general.[71] While in Congress Lynch probably had more influence at the White House than any other Negro has ever had. Grant made him a confidant and in some cases was swayed by Lynch in regard to Southern affairs. Garfield gave him respectful audience in regard to patronage. Yet it is significant that Lynch, in contrast to these presidents, was never suspected of connection with any corrupt transaction of the nature of the Credit Mobilier.[72]

VIRGINIA

As Virginia early passed under Democratic or Conservative control, she was spared much of the race friction of states farther south. There were a few Negroes in the state legislature for twenty years, but they were never strong enough there to cause serious trouble. It seems strange, then, that ten years after Reconstruction ended a Negro was elected to Congress from Virginia for the first and last time. This fact can only be explained in the light of the personality of this remarkable Negro. Since he had already lived sixty years of a most strenuous life, it is necessary to review his earlier career in order to understand the situation.[73]

John Mercer Langston was born December 14, 1829, at Louisa, Virginia. His mother, Lucy, had been a slave but was freed before John's birth. His father was Captain Robert Quarles, his mother's master. Quarles made liberal provisions in his will and arranged that Langston should be taken to Ohio to live.[74]

After his secondary education, Langston graduated from

[71] James G. Blaine, *Twenty Years of Congress*, II, 515; James Ford Rhodes, *op. cit.*, VII, 92.

[72] Lynch, *op. cit.*, p. 147; Jackson *Clarion*, March 17, 1881.

[73] *Journal of Negro History*, VII, 118-119.

[74] John M. Langston, *From A Virginia Plantation to the National Capital*, pp. 11-17.

Oberlin College, both in the literary and theological departments. Studying law privately, he was admitted to the bar and practiced in Oberlin, Ohio. During the war he raised three Negro regiments and after the war he became Inspector General of the Freedmen's Bureau. Leaving this work in 1869, he connected himself with Howard University for seven years, serving respectively as dean of the law department, vice-president and acting president. In 1877 he went to Haiti as minister resident and consul general, remaining there until 1885. At that time he was elected to head the Virginia Normal and Collegiate Institute at Petersburg. When he resigned in 1888 and entered politics, he had been widely known for a generation—an advantage which no previous Negro had in his race for Congress.[75]

Now began one of the longest and most hard fought congressional contests in American history, for it really extended from January 1, 1888, until September 23, 1890. Senator Mahone was Republican "boss" of Virginia and did everything possible to discourage Langston's candidacy, but Langston from the first of the year campaigned steadily. Mahone tried to exclude him from the state convention in May and succeeded, but Langston's friends insisted that he be elected to the national convention, and he was. Then Mahone postponed the fourth district convention until September 19 and tried to control the convention when it met. Mahone dictated the nomination of Arnold, a white man, but the Negroes nominated Langston independently. E. C. Venable was the Democratic candidate.[76]

The district contained eleven counties and every one had a majority of black voters. J. D. Brady, a former Congressman from the district, estimated that nearly ninety-five per cent of the Republicans were Negroes. Consequently it was

[75] *Cong. Directory*, pp. 1202-1203.
[76] Richmond *Dispatch*, February 4, April 25, May 19, September 20, 1888.

good politics for Langston to stress the color line, and he did it to the utmost. But Fred Douglass in response to Mahone's plea entered the fight against Langston and was bitterly denounced for his interference. This open break between these Negro leaders was never healed, for only one of them could be the greatest living Negro.[77]

In desperation the national committee asked Langston to prove the legality of his nomination, but he refused and was branded a bolter. He had the satisfaction of running far ahead of Arnold, but had enabled Venable to win by a plurality.[78] Now the fight was transferred to Congress. Could the Republicans afford to sponsor the cause of an open bolter? But his vote in the House was needed, even if he was an Independent Republican.

Langston lost no chance for publicity during the period of waiting. In February, 1889, he headed a delegation of Negroes to interview President-Elect Harrison. All fifteen Southern and border states were represented, either by persons or by letters. In the autumn Langston campaigned for Mahone, who was running for governor of Virginia. Mahone lost, but Langston had regained favor with the national committee and it could afford to support his contest.[79]

His case was presented early to the Fifty-first Congress, but it was September, 1890, before debate was taken up. The Democrats rested their case on the printed minority report and then absented themselves for nineteen days. They were protesting against Speaker Reed's "tyranny" in general, and against what they considered gross partisanship in this case. The galleries were filled with excited Negroes who saw in Langston the embodiment of all their racial aspirations.

[77] R. L. Morton, "The Negro in Virginia Politics" (Dissertation at University of Virginia, 1918), p. 122, n. 5; Richmond *Dispatch*, August 23 and 24, and September 27, 1888.

[78] Langston, *op. cit.*, p. 455; *Tribune Almanac*, 1889.

[79] Richmond *Dispatch*, February 15, November 1 and 5, 1889.

Finally September 23, 1890, Langston was seated by a vote of 151 to 1, 173 not voting. Haugen and Cannon were very effusive in their joy, and Reed allowed the galleries to hold a wild demonstration.[80]

The following night the Negroes of Washington serenaded Langston, and he responded with a characteristic harangue:

We are now in the great Congress of the nation. We will advance to the Senate and when necessary, when the Negro has grown as great and learned and magnificent as he is now loyal and true, he shall go on to the President's chair. . . . Then a commingling of black men's blood and white men's blood to make our country the grandest on earth.[81]

The *Dispatch* felt impelled to say: "While Langston is one of the best educated men of his race, he is still a Negro with all of a Negro's conceit, pomposity, credulity, and stupidity." [82]

The first session closed within a week, but Langston was present when the second session convened in December. He was appointed to the Education Committee and introduced two bills relating to education. He sought to have a national industrial university for Negroes established by the United States. In proposing popular election of all congressmen and the president, he included a literacy clause for voters. Both bills were referred to committees and ended there.[83]

During this session Langston delivered a long and impressive plea for the Force Bill, but it was saturated with extreme partisanship and racial bias. He contrasted vividly the devoted loyalty of the Negro, and his reward in the form of wholesale proscription. Even whites in Virginia were ostracized for supporting him. Langston was at least frank in his proposed remedies for such conditions:

---

80 Richmond *Dispatch*, September 24, 1890; *Cong. Rec.*, 51st Cong., 1st Sess., pp. 6160, 9822, 10,338.

81 Richmond *Dispatch*, September 26, 1890.

82 *Ibid.*

83 *Cong. Rec.*, 51st Cong., 2nd Sess., pp. 828, 1552, 1650.

Do you like that spirit? I do not. I will never be the coward to say that I do. And I would pass bills and pile up penalties and put behind every bill soldiers until they rose to the top of the mountains and kissed the stars, to put these women and these men in the sure consciousness of their protection by law.[84]

However, his advocacy of a merchant marine subsidy was happily free of his usual bias. In a well-arranged and logical speech he outlined the conditions of the American merchant marine, showed causes of the decline, and suggested encouraging indications for the future. Langston almost adopted a Southern attitude in predicting that Newport News would be a future rival of New York as a port, and that the whole South would share in this prosperity.[85]

Before he was admitted to the Fifty-first Congress, Langston had begun another campaign for the Fifty-second. By August of 1890, Negroes in every county of the fourth district had formally endorsed him and the Force Bill. Mahone ungratefully tried to exclude Langston again and refused to call a district convention, but it met and nominated Langston. Mahone then openly denounced him as unfit, for several reasons. Langston again drew the color line, and it worked, but to his disadvantage. At least he had united the whites solidly in opposition while many Negroes did not vote at all. No white Republican directed his canvass as Brady had in 1888. The natural result was that Epes was elected by the Democrats with a majority of 3,000. Langston made no contest although he charged fraud and bitterly said: "When it comes to the race question the Republicans are all Democrats."[86]

Retiring to private life in Washington, he died there No-

---

[84] *Ibid.*, pp. 1479-1482.

[85] *Ibid.*, pp. 3490-3492.

[86] Richmond *Dispatch*, August 21, and October 9 and 31, 1892; Washington *Post*, November 6, 1892. Mahone charged he was a bolter, a nonresident, and an inciter of race hatred.

vember 15, 1897. Tributes of respect were many and effusive, but the *Times* guardedly styled him "perhaps the most prominent Negro in America." Several colleges and universities had conferred honors on him, and foreign literary and scientific societies had bestowed honorary membership on him. There was agreement that he was the most scholarly of all Negroes who had been in Congress. But even his eulogists admitted that Langston's vanity had detracted from his influence.[87] On the other hand, not only was his influence for good negatived by his bitterness, but also, in the opinion of some, he was directly responsible for a great increase of Negro crime after 1888. Statistics show that there were many Negro rapes of white women with resultant lynchings. Truly this is a heavy indictment, and if just would counterbalance all his brilliancy and eloquence.[88]

NORTH CAROLINA

Hyman had been just another Negro politician, but North Carolina's next Negro congressman was much more adroit. James E. O'Hara was born February 26, 1844, in New York City and shared with Elliott the doubtful distinction of being a black carpetbagger. It is not clear when O'Hara came to North Carolina, but in 1868 he was engrossing clerk of the constitutional convention and then served a term in the legislature, 1868-1869. After studying law in the state and at Howard University, he was admitted to the bar in 1873. In 1875 he was one of six Negroes in the constitutional convention. He was chairman of the board of commissioners of Halifax County, 1872-1876.[89]

By 1878 O'Hara was ready for a wider field of activity. He ran for Congress in the second district and claimed to

---

[87] New York *Times*, November 16, 1897; Ferris, *op. cit.*, II, 745.

[88] Morton, *op. cit.*, pp. 128, 137.

[89] *Cong. Directory*, p. 1369; Hamilton, *op. cit.*, p. 637.

have been elected, but the certificate of election was given to William H. Kitchin. The *National Republican* felt that he did not have a fair chance:

The Republicans in the second Congressional district of North Carolina might as well vote in Borneo for all the good it will do them in the election of candidates to office. The Democratic canvassing boards perform every kind of atrocity known to the bulldozing Democratic politician, even to defying the courts.[90]

He was more successful, however, in 1882, for the Democrats made no effective opposition, and he won by a tremendous vote of 18,351 against a scattering opposition vote of 1,413. This was a Democratic House to which he was elected, and for several months O'Hara was the only Negro in Congress. But E. W. M. Mackey of South Carolina died in January, 1884, and was succeeded by Smalls. It was significant that no white man would report the death of this notorious scalawag and it fell to O'Hara's lot to do so. He submitted the usual resolutions of respect and was appointed on the Funeral Committee.[91]

He held membership also on the Mines and Mining and on the Expenditures on Public Buildings Committees. O'Hara introduced a number of bills, but they were mainly of a private or local nature. As the Civil Rights Bill had been declared null and void, however, O'Hara proposed a constitutional amendment relative to civil rights, but his joint resolution died in committee.

During the spring and summer of 1884, he was granted leaves of absence aggregating forty-nine days. Sometimes the reason was given as important business, and at other times no explanation was offered. As he had no contest pending, this

[90] *Cong. Directory*, p. 1369; *National Republican*, December 30, 1878.
[91] *Tribune Almanac*, 1883; *Cong. Rec.*, 48th Cong., 1st Sess., p. 710.

appears to be a neglect of public business for the sake of private business.[92]

O'Hara was more at ease in the next session and pursued further the civil rights issue. He proposed a bill to give Negroes rights equal to those of the whites in Washington restaurants, but no action was taken on it. In his main fight of the session he was more successful. Reagan's bill regulating interstate commerce was before the House when O'Hara secured an amendment to the effect that equal accommodations must be provided for all without discrimination. Other clauses were inserted to allow railroads to classify passengers for public comfort and safety but with no discrimination on account of race or color, and so O'Hara had won his point after all. He had stated his motive as follows:

Mr. Speaker, this is not class legislation. I do not nor would I ask such. It is not a race question nor is it a political action. It rises far above all these. It is plain healthy legislation strictly in keeping with the enlightened sentiment and spirit of the age in which we live; it is legislation looking to and guarding the rights of every citizen of this great Republic however humble may be his station in our social scale.[93]

In this meticulous regard for equal rights, O'Hara sometimes went to an unnecessary length. He asked for an amendment to the Pension Appropriation Bill providing that the same mode and manner of payment should apply to all. Randall thought that was the law already, but no one could object; it was passed without a record vote.[94]

The Goldsboro *Messenger*, intimating that O'Hara was only putting in time and doing nothing for it, said: "O'Hara draws his pay with the regularity with which the animal without hope of posterity walks to his hay and fodder." At any

[92] *Ibid.*, pp. 224, 282, *passim.*
[93] *Ibid.*, 2nd Sess., pp. 805, 296-298, 315-317.
[94] *Ibid.*, p. 501.

rate, he was active in his district, for in 1884 at the state convention he received the highest vote for delegate-at-large to the national convention. O'Hara made an attack on Democracy during this state convention but it was mild compared to P. H. Winston's virulent speech. After the convention he issued an address to all in the state opposed to Democracy. He recounted the horrors of Southern outrages but weakened his case by concluding with a tame appeal to subscribe to the *National Republican.* The *News and Courier* thought: "It looks like small business for even such a Congressman to turn out as a canvassing agent for a weekly paper and such a paper!" [95]

The Democrats made a fight this time in the second district but with no hope of winning. They considered it a glorious victory in November when they carried every district except O'Hara's and cut his majority to 6,700.[96] It is noticeable that the main Democratic paper, the *News and Observer,* ran a column every day headed "North Carolina in Congress." This was a daily record of what they did and how they voted, and no distinction was made of O'Hara, nor was his color mentioned.[97]

O'Hara's principal support in this Congress was given to the fight for dependent and private pensions, in opposition to President Cleveland's vetoes. O'Hara argued that the country was wealthy enough to afford and would not feel the extra burden. Time after time he voted to override the veto.[98]

But his best speech of this congress was in opposition to the oleomargarine tax bill. He contended this bill would require extra offices to reward party favorites. As strange as it seemed, he yet put up a plea for states rights, contending that the legis-

---

[95] Raleigh *News and Observer,* April 5, 1884, quoting Goldsboro *Messenger,* and May 2, 1884; Charleston *News and Courier,* May 5, 1884.

[96] Raleigh *News and Observer,* November 6, 1884; *Tribune Almanac,* 1885.

[97] Raleigh *News and Observer,* issues of 1885.

[98] *Cong. Rec.,* 49th Cong., 1st Sess., p. 6030; 2nd Sess., *passim.*

latures should be allowed to handle the situation. The proposed bill, he claimed, would create an army of Jean Valjeans to follow with sleuth-hound tenacity every imaginary violator of the law. The Democrats had protested against taxes for ten years and now, he charged, they were increasing taxes.[99] Again it all depended on whose ox was gored.

The very size of the Republican majority in the second district led to overconfidence and internal jealousy. In 1886 some of the Negroes preferred a black man to one of a gingercake color. They nominated Abbott, a coal black Negro, but O'Hara insisted on running also. This gave F. M. Simmons, the Democratic nominee, a good opportunity, which he utilized to advantage. It was reported at Warrenton that he made the best speech heard there since the war. The natural result of a Republican split followed. Simmons received 15,128 votes; O'Hara came next with a vote of 13,060; Abbott last with 5,020.[100]

O'Hara resumed his law practice in Newbern and did not enter politics again. He remained in Newbern until his death, September 15, 1905.[101]

The next Negro sent to Congress from North Carolina, in contrast with O'Hara, was a native and always identified himself with the better class of white people. Henry Plummer Cheatham was born December 27, 1857, near Henderson. Cheatham was born a slave but, as his mother was a house maid on a large plantation, he experienced none of the hardships of slavery. On the other hand, he remembered with affection his old master's family, and extended favors to them whenever possible. After the war he attended public schools taught by ex-slaveholders. Then he attended the preparatory and college departments at Shaw University, graduating there

[99] *Ibid.*, 1st Sess., pp. 5163-5164.
[100] Raleigh *News and Observer*, September 1 and October 17, 1886.
[101] *Cong. Directory*, p. 1369.

in 1883. He read law but never practiced. After a year of teaching, he was elected register of deeds for Vance County, and served two terms in this position, 1884-1888.[102]

Having this preliminary public experience, Cheatham had become the logical candidate for Congress in 1888. However, again there was discord among the Republicans, and after Cheatham's nomination George Mebane also insisted on running. This would be disastrous, as Simmons had been renominated unanimously and would be stronger than in 1886. So by September Mebane was persuaded to retire, being bought off, the Democrats alleged. At any rate the Republican breach was healed, while Simmons was held late in Congress and could not make an effective canvass. In addition Cheatham was an effective campaigner and believed that many Democrats voted for him. He was a very fluent speaker, possessed an extensive vocabulary and a forceful expression. While capable of appealing to whites, he also was shrewd in adapting himself to Negro psychology. Consequently, he was able to counteract Simmons' good record in Congress and to beat him by a close vote of 16,704 to 16,051.[103]

When the Fifty-first Congress was organized December 2, 1889, Cheatham was present, and he was the only Negro until Langston and Miller were seated in September, 1890. This made him the spokesman of the 7,000,000 of his race, but he played the role in a moderate and restrained manner. He introduced a bill for relief of the depositors of the Freedmen's Bank, but this was generally considered an act of justice and not a racial matter. Although he voted for the Force Bill, he did it reluctantly and explained out of Congress: "I have both races in my district. I want to cast my vote for that law which will be best not for one race or the other but for both equally." He felt compelled to stand by the caucus de-

---

[102] *Ibid.*, p. 805. The author interviewed H. P. Cheatham, August, 1929.
[103] Personal interview; Richmond *Dispatch*, September 22, 1888.

cision but within that limit threw his influence to modera-
tion.[104]

In behalf of all his constituents he opposed the tax on oleomargarine. His remarks relative to this showed the heavy
burden that would be imposed on Negro and white small
farmers. The Negroes were at last prospering, having recov-
ered, he claimed, from the deception of Northern whites.
These, Cheatham said, had proved false in nine cases out of
ten, and even the Freedmen's Bureau had exploited the
Negro.[105]

His nonpartisan interest was also shown in a bill he introduced to aid in the establishment and temporary support of
public schools. A special order was given his bill on the calendar, but other business crowded in, and the bill did not
come to a vote.[106]

By 1890 the restlessness of the American farmers was very
great, and party lines were breaking. The farmers in the
second North Carolina district wanted a farmer to represent
them, and that militated against the candidacy of Simmons,
a lawyer. J. M. Mewborne was a candidate for the Democratic
nomination but "Delegate" wrote to the *News and Observer*
that Mewborne was not a good Democrat, and that it would
require a strong man to defeat Cheatham. Consequently,
Rogers was nominated, but, as he became seriously ill, the
Democrats just before election accepted Mewborne. This
Democratic uncertainty aided Cheatham, and he won by 1,200
majority.[107]

In the Fifty-second Congress, Cheatham was again the
only Negro. Therefore, he introduced a bill for an appropria-

[104] *Cong. Rec.*, 51st Cong., 1st Sess., pp. 248, 6940; Raleigh *News and Observer*,
May 14, 1890.

[105] *Cong. Rec.*, 51st Cong., 1st Sess., Appendix, p. 624.

[106] *Ibid.*, 1st Sess., p. 248; 2nd Sess., p. 2830.

[107] Raleigh *News and Observer*, July 29, August 3, September 3, and October 25,
1890; *World Almanac*, 1891.

tion to show Negro progress in an exhibit at the Columbian Exposition. Another bill of his concerned the preparation of statistics relative to the colored race. The House was Democratic, but Cheatham denied any political motive and hoped the majority could grant his request. For as he reminded the House: "I have taken but little of your time, I have said but little this session." [108]

Speaking for a tax on options and futures, Cheatham went outside his district and showed interest in the bulk of Southern people who were engaged in agriculture. He believed such a bill would enable the small farmers to realize a fair price on their products.[109]

Cheatham was absent on leave on account of sickness during most of his next and final session. The introduction of two private bills constituted his only attempt at legislation.[110]

This closed his record in Congress—not an impressive one, but creditable and serviceable. Cheatham realized his limitations and sought to do more in the committee room and by personal contact than in set speeches on the floor. He was friendly with all members, even Democrats and Southerners. Among his personal friends were numbered McKinley, Lodge, Cannon, Reed, Dingley, Holman, Kilgore, and Crisp. Several Democrats were kept in federal office by his influence. An incident concerning his old mistress shows his respect for his former master's family. Meeting her one day when she was driving in Washington, Cheatham climbed into the phaeton and drove her to the Capitol.[111]

He was the Republican nominee in 1892 and 1894 but was beaten both times by F. A. Woodard. He was Recorder of Deeds, 1897-1901, for the District of Columbia. Then he

[108] *Cong. Rec.*, 52nd Cong., 1st Sess., pp. 4695, 4740, 6824.
[109] *Ibid.*, Appendix, pp. 508-510.
[110] *Ibid.*, 2nd Sess., pp. 185, 840, 1085.
[111] Interview with H. P. Cheatham; interview with W. T. Page, Clerk of the House, November, 1929.

moved to Oxford, North Carolina. After 1907 he served as president of a Negro orphanage. He brought this institution into a high state of excellence by his energy and resourcefulness. When he died, November 29, 1935, his passing was mourned by multitudes of white friends as well as by his own race. His funeral was attended by leading white officials of the state.[112]

The next and last North Carolina Negro to serve in Congress was a man of quite a different type from Cheatham. George H. White was born a slave, December 18, 1852, at Rosindale, North Carolina. After a public school education, he attended Howard University, graduating there in 1877. He studied law and was licensed in 1879 to practice in all courts of the state. From 1880 to 1884 he was a member of the legislature; from 1886 to 1894 he was solicitor of the second judicial district.[113]

As Cheatham had definitely retired, White became the outstanding Negro in the district and was nominated in 1896. The Populist movement was at its height in North Carolina, and White reaped the advantage of it, as, for the time, the Populists had fused with the Republicans. This worked to give White a 3,900 majority over Woodard, the Democratic incumbent.[114]

Entering the Fifty-fifth Congress in 1897, for four years White was the only Negro in Congress. Also the relentless logic of events showed that he would be the last one for a long time. White, having a flair for the dramatic, gladly seized and used to the utmost his role as sole spokesman for 9,000,000 people. When Langston died, in November, 1897, White became his successor as a bitter, uncompromising assailant of everything that resembled or could be distorted

[112] *World Almanac*, 1893, 1895; Oxford *Public Ledger*, December 3, 1935.
[113] *Cong. Directory*, p. 1690.
[114] Raleigh *News and Observer*, November 6, 1896; *World Almanac*, 1897.

into racial discrimination. No matter what the topic under discussion might be, White, like Cato of Rome, could always bring it around to a discussion of Negro rights. Long experience as a solicitor had made him an easy, fluent speaker, and his speeches are very readable.

McKinley had called a special session, and within its first month White made a strong argument in support of the pending Dingley tariff. He justified his attitude by saying:

I am here to speak and I do speak as the sole representative on this floor of 9,000,000 of the population of these United States, 90% of whom are laborers. Under this bill they are protected; they are given an opportunity to earn their living. Bread and butter are what we want, not finespun Democratic campaign theory.[115]

In the next session, White proclaimed himself as frank spoilsman: "I proclaim it as my doctrine, that to the victor belong the spoils; or in language a little more primitive, if you please, the ox that pulls the plow ought to have a chance to eat the fodder." [116]

White was the only Negro to serve in Congress during a war. As it was seen to be inevitable by March, 1898, White took a bold patriotic stand and pledged a "half million strong black phalanx" for national defense. He asked that one of two new artillery regiments be a Negro one, but this was rejected. April 19 he rose for a personal explanation, saying he had traveled 450 miles the day before to vote for intervention in Cuba, but reached Washington too late. He was present April 25 when war was declared, but no record vote was taken. However, on every other defense measure White is recorded in its favor.[117]

With the war ended, White again took strong ground on the alleged suppression of Negro votes in the South, and

[115] *Cong. Rec.*, 55th Cong., 1st Sess., pp. 550-551.
[116] *Ibid.*, 2nd Sess., pp. 541-542.
[117] *Ibid.*, pp. 2556, 4086, *passim.*

rged reduction of representation accordingly. He reminded
he House that the Negro had progressed wonderfully. The
ollowing passage became famous:

We are passing . . . from ignorance to intelligence. No race
as made greater progress in a given time. We are entitled to your
ecognition. We do not ask for domination. We ask and expect a
hance in legislation and will be content with nothing else. . . . You
an not always keep a free man down.[118]

White could be nonpartisan sometimes, but such occasions
vere the exception. W. W. Kitchin was attempting to secure
new federal building for Durham, and White came to his
upport and showed his state pride. He predicted that Durham
vould become one of the greatest sources of federal revenue
n the South. But the unusual alliance of Kitchin and White
vas defeated on this point.[119]

In the summer of 1898 White was a candidate for re-
lection. The United States was still officially at war, but that
lid not prevent a bitter campaign throughout North Carolina.
White was as aggressive as ever, and the whites had reached
point where they detested him. Negroes were holding many
ocal and county offices in the east, and White asserted they
vould hold more in the future. It was also irritating when he
eviewed and addressed the Third North Carolina Regiment,
officered by Negroes from Colonel Young down. The Demo-
rats made no nomination but supported the Populist, Lloyd.
But this attempted new fusion was not successful, and White
von by a 2,600 majority.[120]

During the Fifty-sixth Congress, White was more race
onscious than ever. Consequently he was frequently in a quar-
el, either in Congress or out. January 31, 1900, he made

[118] *Ibid.*, 3rd Sess., pp. 1124-1126.
[119] *Ibid.*, pp. 2894-2895.
[120] Raleigh *News and Observer*, September 2, 7, 8, and 10, and December 3,
898.

an offensive statement on the floor which played a part in the campaign just opening in North Carolina. White said only fifteen per cent of lynchings were caused by rape of white women and added: "And there are many more outrages against colored women by white men than there are by colored men against white women." The *News and Observer* replied: "White is typical of his kind, venomous, forward, slanderous of the whites, appealing to the worst passions of his own race, he emphasizes anew the need of making an end of him and his kind." [121]

Not content with this mental battle, White stirred up another. He introduced a bill making lynching a federal crime, and spoke at length in defense of it. This was a forerunner of later similar bills, but White's was more severe, for it would make all aiding and abetting lynching guilty of treason. [122]

In his last session he secured transfer of $100,000 unclaimed by Negro soldiers, to be used for a home for aged and infirm Negroes in Washington. [123] Then, as the session drew to a close, White delivered the Negroes' valedictory to Congress. It would have been an excellent one had the note of bitterness not been so strong. Always, in White's estimation, the white race was in the wrong and the Negro, the innocent victim. His conclusion has often been quoted:

This, Mr. Chairman, is perhaps the Negroes' temporary farewell to the American Congress; but let me say Phoenix-like he will rise up some day and come again. These parting words are in behalf of an outraged, heart-broken, bruised and bleeding, but God-fearing people, faithful, industrial, loyal people, rising people, full of potential force. . . . The only apology that I have to make

[121] *Cong. Rec.*, 56th Cong., 1st Sess., pp. 1365, 1507. White had the *News and Observer* comment read into the record in order to deny that he had incited crime.
[122] *Ibid.*, pp. 1021, 2151-2154.
[123] *Ibid.*, 2nd Sess., pp. 1268-1271.

for the earnestness with which I have spoken is that I am pleading for the life, the liberty, the future happiness, and manhood suffrage for one-eighth of the entire population of the United States.[124]

White was not a candidate in 1900. The state constitutional amendment qualifying the suffrage had passed in August. It would not become effective until 1902, but White saw that the Negro's career in politics was over. A white Republican was nominated and George White took little part in his canvass. Every county in the district went Democratic. When noon, March 4, 1901, was reached both houses of the legislature took official notice that White's term had ended, and speeches of thanksgiving were uttered. He retired to Philadelphia and practiced law until his death, December 28, 1918.[125]

[124] *Ibid.*, p. 1638 f.
[125] Raleigh *News and Observer*, September 14, 18, December 1, 1900, and March 5, 1901; *Cong. Directory*, p. 1690.

V

UNSUCCESSFUL NEGRO ASPIRANTS FOR CONGRESS

It is obviously impossible to prepare an exhaustive list of all Negro candidates for Congress during the period under survey. Nearly all the unsuccessful candidates were comparatively obscure. They usually ran as Independent Republicans, and, without the influence and financial support of the party organization, they had small chance of victory. Langston was the unusual case of winning against the organization, but even he compromised to get his seat.[1]

There is no record of a Negro Democrat being nominated for Congress in this period. On rare occasions, however, the Democrats or Conservatives made no nomination and supported a Negro as the lesser of two evils. This will be noted especially in the case of Samuel Lee. It is of significance, also, that in the period being considered no Negro was sent to Congress from the North, nor was one ever nominated until 1928.[2]

It would be profitless to discuss the campaigns of all these nonentities, for most of them returned to the obscurity from which they had temporarily emerged. On the other hand, it

[1] *Supra,* pp. 113-115.

[2] Letter from Oscar DePriest to the author, January 10, 1930. DePriest, elected from Illinois in 1928, is the first Negro congressman from the North. In 1882, 25,000 Negro voters in Kansas asked that the Reverend A. Fairfax be put on the ticket for congressman-at-large. The Republican state convention refused to consider it. (Jackson *Clarion,* July 12, 1882.)

is proposed to give attention to a few outstanding Negro contestants, and then merely to sketch others less important.

When the Fortieth Congress met in December, 1868, a Negro presented himself for membership in the House, two years before Rainey was admitted. There had arisen a vacancy in the second Louisiana district, and J. Willis Menard of New Orleans was given a certificate of election by Governor Warmoth. But Caleb S. Hunt, a white man, contested, and the House settled the matter by rejecting both and leaving the seat vacant. Yet Menard was allowed to plead his case on the floor and thus had the distinction of being the first Negro to speak to Congress. Menard was a college graduate and would have made a good representative of the race, but the Radicals feared the country was not ready for such a step.[3]

His treatment may explain why, several years later in Florida, Menard bolted the ticket and ran for Congress as an Independent. He charged that the Republicans had outraged the Negroes and excluded them from nominations. He, however, received a very small vote. In the same manner he approved of Hayes's moderate policy, saying eight years of bayonet rule had failed.[4]

Probably the most interesting Negro in Reconstruction also belonged to the Louisiana group. P. B. S. Pinchback, born in 1837, was the son of a wealthy planter who had him educated at a private school in Cincinnati. During the war he raised a Negro company and was its captain. After the war he had a remarkable political career for twenty years, during which time he held more offices than any other Negro in the United States. Within the party he was a member of the state executive committee and a frequent delegate to the national con-

---

[3] McClure, *op. cit.*, p. 252; *Cong. Directory*, p. 296, n. 5.

[4] Jacksonville *Florida Union*, October 5 and November 9, 1876; Jacksonville *Floridian*, August 27, 1877.

ventions. But to serve in a wider field his party elected him to the constitutional convention, to the legislature, to the offices of lieutenant-governor and president of the senate, and claimed he was elected as congressman-at-large and as United States senator. He held, also, the following appointive offices: member state board of education, trustee of Southern University, collector of customs, and state commissioner to the Vienna Exposition. It is true that he was rejected by both Houses of Congress, but his contests won him prestige and about $20,000 for expenses. In 1876, while he was waiting in Washington, the New York *Commercial Advertiser* remarked that he was the best dressed Southern man in Congress since the days when gentlemen were Democrats.[5]

In business he was very successful, for besides ordinary occupations he was deeply involved in lotteries and race track gambling. By 1900 it was estimated that he had an annual income of $10,000. As a business man he approved of Cleveland's election in 1884 and hastened to reassure the Negroes that they must not believe Blaine's charges of disaster under Democratic rule.[6]

Another member of the Louisiana group was James Lewis, who held a colonel's commission in the militia. In 1872 he was nominated for congressman-at-large but, finding a breach had been made in party harmony, he withdrew in favor of Pinchback. When Pinchback was rejected by the Senate, Lewis was elected to the vacancy, but, as the state was being turned over to the Democrats, Lewis did not press his claim before the Senate. Like many other politicians, he and Pinchback retired to Washington for their last days.[7]

An influential Negro in North Carolina politics for twenty

[5] Simmons, *op. cit.*, pp. 759-774.

[6] *Ibid.*, p. 774; New York *Times*, November 23, 1884.

[7] Simmons, *op. cit.*, p. 956. Whitfield McKinlay, a Negro from South Carolina who moved to Washington, knew these men well and furnished information concerning them to the author, November, 1929.

years was James H. Harris. He had been educated in Ohio but returned to North Carolina in 1865 and at once became active in organizing the Negroes. In 1868 he was twice nominated for Congress for both long and short terms, but John T. Deweese, a carpetbagger, paid him both times to withdraw. In 1870 no one would buy him off, but he was defeated by S. H. Rogers. Harris contested and was rejected by Congress but was solaced with $1,500 for expenses.[8]

Although Harris was not nominated again, he continued a power in the party. He was called "the shrewd leader of the darkies" and the "great colored orator of North Carolina," by his enemies and admirers, respectively. In 1882 he challenged Governor Jarvis to a joint debate on the campaign issues, but Jarvis ignored him. Harris remained popular in the party as late as 1886. Old citizens remember him as a tall, slim, forceful man, and considered him an effective, interesting orator. Although Harris was a strong partisan and was fond of denouncing the Bourbon Democracy, he is not considered as venomous as George White.[9]

Samuel Lee, Independent Republican of Sumter, South Carolina, had the unusual experience of being supported by the whites in 1874 in preference to Rainey. The *News and Courier* estimated that 9,000 whites would vote for him and that he would have a chance to beat Rainey. The *News and Courier* called him an honest man and a reformer, and said that he deserved Conservative votes. Evidently he received 8,000 Democratic votes, as he lost by less than 1,000 votes. He contested in the Forty-fourth Congress and was given $1,200 for expenses.[10]

---

[8] Hamilton, *op. cit.*, pp. 281, 285, 493; *Cong. Globe*, 42nd Cong., 2nd Sess., p. 3086.

[9] The author interviewed S. A. Ashe, C. B. Edwards, and Josephus Daniels, May, 1929, at Raleigh, North Carolina.

[10] Charleston *News and Courier*, October 15, 28, and December 1, 1874; *Cong. Rec.*, 44th Cong., 2nd Sess., p. 1560.

By 1880 Lee had come back into the fold and was the regular Republican nominee against Captain Richardson. Apparently his character had changed, also, for it is disclosed that he was guilty of malfeasance when a probate judge. True to form, he contested in the Forty-seventh Congress. Then partisanship played Lee a strange trick. On the last day of the last session, the Republicans voted Richardson out, but the Democrats filibustered and refused to vote on the resolution to admit Lee. As there was no quorum, Lee lost his expected $10,000.[11]

Besides these few men who were almost successful, there were many more who had no chance of election. The table on the facing page shows their distribution by state and year. All of these sought election to the House of Representatives.[12]

It was rare indeed when a Negro aspired to the United States Senate. But in 1870 James J. Spelman received several votes in the Mississippi legislature before Revels was finally chosen. He was a carpetbagger from Connecticut who came to Mississippi in 1868. Nothing is known of him after this.[13]

It appears from the records that the last Negro candidate from the South was Aaron P. Prioleau in the election of 1914. Prioleau was the Republican candidate in the first South Carolina district. Contesting before the Sixty-fourth Congress, he was refused the seat by the unanimous committee report, and the House, July 21, 1916, adopted the report without discussion.[14]

No Negro has been elected to Congress in the South since 1898. There are several reasons for this. One of the main reasons is the practical disappearance of the Negro vote after

[11] Charleston *News and Courier*, September 29, 1880, and March 4, 1883.

[12] Table compiled from data taken from New York *Times* and from local newspapers in the respective states. In the case of some obscure characters the given name is not obtainable.

[13] Simmons, *op. cit.*, p. 928.

[14] *Cong. Rec.*, 64th Cong., 1st Sess., p. 11,400.

YEAR	CANDIDATE	STATE
1870	Ed Shaw	Tennessee
1870	——— Houston	Georgia
1870	——— Bradley	Georgia
1870	R. W. White	Georgia
1870	——— Beard	Georgia
1870	* Lucius Wimbush	South Carolina
1872	* Joseph Quash	South Carolina
1874	Robert Meacham	Florida
1874	——— Harrison	Georgia
1880	——— Witherspoon	Florida
1882	H. C. Carter	Mississippi
1882	Joseph Hill	Mississippi
1884	E. H. Deas	South Carolina
1884	E. J. Dickerson	South Carolina
1884	——— Evans	Virginia
1886	——— Abbott	North Carolina
1890	——— Moore	North Carolina
1890	John Mitchell	Virginia
1890	——— Crum	South Carolina
1890	——— Smith	South Carolina
1890	——— Levy	South Carolina
1890	E. H. Deas	South Carolina
1892	——— Williamson	North Carolina

* Unsuccessful candidate for congressman-at-large.

this time. It was seen that the old Reconstruction methods of eliminating the Negro vote must be replaced by legal and permanent methods. So laws were passed restricting the suffrage and yet conforming to the United States Constitution and the state constitutions. Such laws were passed by Mississippi in 1890; South Carolina, 1895; Louisiana, 1898; North Carolina, 1900; Alabama and Virginia, 1901; Georgia, 1908; and Oklahoma, 1910. These laws restrict the suffrage by requiring payment of taxes, or ownership of property, or ability to read and understand, or a fixed residence for a year or two years. They have stood the test of the federal courts and so they are proved legal and yet effective. The statement is often made that these laws are manipulated to allow all whites to vote. Nothing could be more erroneous, for tens of thousands of whites are disqualified. On the other hand, many Negroes still vote, even in South Carolina. But as a whole these laws and new state constitutions have secured a white electorate, and white voters always elect white candidates to Congress.[15]

The Negro vote, moreover, had dropped sharply, even before these restrictions. There was a change of 10,000 votes in 1900 in the second North Carolina district before the regulation went into force.[16]

Negro leaders capable of serving in Congress were not being produced. The Negroes, soon after the Civil War, had the guardianship of the federal government; now they had to stand on their own feet. Booker T. Washington said that those early Negro congressmen were the aristocracy of the race. Like the white aristocrats, they had the Southern ideal that a gentleman must take part in politics. Later on they saw there was a better chance in business and left politics.[17]

[15] Jerome Dowd, *The Negro in American Life,* pp. 105 f., and also author's personal observation in South Carolina.

[16] Raleigh *News and Observer,* December 1, 1900.

[17] Booker T. Washington, *The Story of the Negro,* II, 193.

VI

CONCLUSIONS AND EVALUATIONS

THERE ARE A number of conflicting opinions as to whether the Negro accomplished anything in Congress, and if not, why he failed. Negro historians and writers, such as Woodson, Taylor, and Andrews, are usually reliable in their facts, but their interpretations are not justified by the facts. They insist that no shortcomings of the Negro in politics are due to him, but always they are explained by the unfairness of the white man. On the other hand, white historians, writers, and statesmen, are almost a unit in agreeing that the Negro failed in Congress and that at least a part of the blame was inherent. It is proposed, therefore, to consider contemporary and later opinions, and to endeavor to reach an approximately accurate evaluation of the services of these Negro congressmen.

R. B. Elliott said:

I can bear defeat but the humiliation this thing has brought on our race—that's what hurts me. . . . The report has gone to the world that the colored legislators . . . have been bribed by the wholesale and the report is unfortunately true. What will the world think of it? [1]

Roger A. Pryor wrote: "We have not yet heard that a Negro congressman was in any way implicated in the Credit Mobilier scandal." [2]

[1] Mobile *Register*, February 14, 1873, refers to his senatorial race.
[2] Montgomery *Journal*, December 25, 1873.

Representative Robbins of North Carolina said on the floor of Congress:

Sir, the Negro is a clinging parasite. He looks up to others as his superiors. . . . Even here on this floor (and I mean no disrespect to any fellow member by this remark) he does nothing, he says nothing except as he is prompted by his managers; even here he obeys the bidding of his new white masters, who move him like a puppet on the chess board. . . . He is the world's merry Andrew . . . but when you come to grand tragic and heroic parts . . . the Negro fails.[3]

The *National Republican* was pro-Negro, and yet in a column headed "Colored Demagogues" it denounced the disgraceful sessions of the Equal Rights Convention, meeting in Washington. Rainey, Ransier, Cain, Elliott, Rapier, Lynch, and Walls were all active in the convention, but the *Republican* said that the proceedings disgusted the law-abiding onlooker of either race and gave ground to the Democratic claim that the Negroes were unfitted for their new privileges. "A pair of eye glasses, an arrogant, overbearing manner, a few book learned phrases, and a modern suit of clothing do not fill the requirements of leadership." [4]

Representative Townsend of New York complimented his Negro colleagues:

These men during the time I have sat here have come into this hall well-dressed, they assume the carriage of gentlemen; they insult no one; they encroach upon no man; and in the few instances in which they have risen to address the House, it has been done with an intelligence, a deference and consideration that might do credit to any statesman in the land.[5]

The Charleston *News and Courier* said: "Colored Congressmen have no earthly influence in Washington, even

---

[3] *Cong. Rec.*, 43rd Cong., 1st Sess., p. 898.
[4] *National Republican*, April 6, 1874.
[5] Jacksonville *Daily Florida Union*, February 3, 1876.

among Republicans. They are voting machines and nothing more." [6]

The New Orleans *Republican*, when there were seven Negroes in Congress, including Senator Bruce, said: "There does not seem to be one Republican member of either branch of Congress ... who represents with ability the Republicans of the South. The Republicans of the South should hasten to correct the unfortunate error of committing their interests to persons incompetent to defend them." [7]

In 1884 the white Republicans of Georgia issued an address:

We have now in Georgia ten Congressional districts and in several of them the Negroes have a numerical majority. Yet no sensible man can foster the least hope that under Negro leadership a Republican Congressman can be elected in either of them. We have tried Negroes as party leaders for sixteen years and find them totally inefficient. They in general are not reliable voters, they are utterly incompetent as leaders, and they have no capacity whatever for organization. [8]

The New York *Enterprise*, a Negro paper, admitted in 1886 that the first experience of Negroes with representatives of their own color proved that it was better to have white men to represent them. Smalls and O'Hara were denounced by name as demagogues. [9]

In 1888 when Langston was making his race in Virginia, attention was drawn to the anomaly that no Northern state even nominated a Negro, much less elected one. Yet the Negro held the balance of power in several states. In a political sense the North was using him only as a hewer of wood

[6] Charleston *News and Courier*, September 13, 1876.
[7] New Orleans *Republican*, February 7, 1877.
[8] Washington *Post*, April 5, 1884.
[9] Charleston *News and Courier*, November 9, 1886, quoting New York *Enterprise*.

and drawer of water.[10] But Fred Douglass, the arch enemy of anything Southern, had publicly admitted this as early as 1879, when urging the Negroes not to move to Kansas:

By staying where they are they may be able to send abler, better, and more effective representatives of their race to Congress. In the South the Negro has at least the possibility of power; in the North he has no such possibility, and it is for him to say how well he can afford to part with this possible power.[11]

In spite of the membership of the scholarly Langston, Senator Pugh in 1890 observed on the floor of the Senate:

I have read some of their [Negro Congressmen] speeches on various subjects and they struck me as being characterized by intelligence and ability. I think that the colored Representatives from the South, as a rule, so far as my knowledge extends, have been men of fair ability and intelligence. . . . The Negro is an imitative being and absorbs knowledge mostly by observation and association. . . . I do not know of a single one . . . elected to the House of Representatives who was not educated, raised, trained, and made what he was by white association and white influence, by white training.[12]

Blaine said:

The colored man . . . in due season was sent to Congress. Did harm result from it? Nay, was it not the needed demonstration of the freedom and justice of a republican government? If it be viewed simply as an experiment, it was triumphantly successful. The colored men who took seats in both Senate and House, did not appear ignorant or helpless. They were as a rule studious, earnest, ambitious men whose public conduct—as illustrated by Mr. Revels and Mr. Bruce in the Senate, and Mr. Rapier, Mr. Lynch, and Mr. Rainey in the House—would be honorable to any race. Coals of

[10] Richmond *Dispatch*, February 14, 1888, quoting Representative Hemphill.
[11] Carter G. Woodson, *Negro Orators and Their Orations*, p. 469.
[12] *Cong. Rec.*, 51st Cong., 2nd Sess., p. 78.

fire were heaped on the heads of all their enemies in removing the disabilities of those who have been their oppressors and who have continued to treat them with injustice and ignominy.[18]

This is very favorable comment from one well qualified to speak. The omission of Elliott's name, however, is significant.

Rhodes wrote: "They [Negro Congressmen] left no mark on the legislation of their time; none of them in comparison with their white associates, attained the least distinction." He noted that none were elected from the North and concluded: "In a word he [the Negro] has been politically a failure and he could not have been otherwise." [14]

Fleming asserted: "Revels, Lynch, and Bruce represent the better Negro office holders; Pinchback, Rainey, and Nash, the less respectable ones; and below these were the rascals whose ambition was to equal their white preceptors in corruption." [15]

Paul L. Dunbar was proud of his race, but said of its congressmen: "The illiterate and inefficient black man whom circumstances put into Congress was a representative but was not representative. To have achieved something for the betterment of his race rather than for the aggrandizement of himself, seems to be a man's best title to be called representative." [16] On another occasion, in lighter vein, Dunbar said: "Some men are born great, some achieve greatness, and others lived during the Reconstruction period." [17]

Booker T. Washington thought that, outside of a few lead-

[18] Blaine, op. cit., II, 515.

[14] Rhodes, op. cit., VII, 169-170. Quoted by permission of The Macmillan Company.

[15] From "The Sequel of Appomattox," Volume 32, The Chronicles of America (copyright Yale University Press), p. 242 and note. Fleming, to show his indifference to the Negroes in Congress states that there were only fifteen in Congress, thus overlooking seven altogether.

[16] Jerome Dowd, The Negro in American Life, p. 511. Quoted by permission of D. Appleton-Century Company.

[17] Reuter, The Mulatto in the United States, p. 249. Quoted by permission of Chapman and Grimes, Inc.

ers, Negroes had very little influence on the course of events in Reconstruction, that it was a white man's quarrel, and that the Negro was the tennis ball. He felt all the time that Negro office-holding was an unstable condition that could not last.[18]

Woodson says that, with the exception of Elliott, the great orators of the day were not in Congress. "While most of the Negroes who served in that body were as a rule abler than the average white member," they were not always equal to the Negroes who did not engage in politics.[19]

A. A. Taylor, a professional Negro investigator, explains why the Negro failed to secure any legislation but consumed his efforts on racial and local measures. National measures, he said, were formulated by seasoned veterans. Also, the Negroes were too weak to secure the passage of racial measures, and the white Republicans would not co-operate with them. Therefore, he claimed, their failure was not an evidence of lack of ability and statesmanship.[20] Evidently Taylor forgot the long service of Rainey and Smalls, and his very defense convicts the Negro congressman of ineffectiveness.

In like manner, N. P. Andrews solves the difficulty by charging Hamilton, Burgess, and others, with being prejudiced and dismisses them all with: "Of these radical utterances, historians need take little notice. They are of value here for the reason that they show the lack of scientific Reconstruction history." [21]

Of interest are comments by Murray and Cheatham after they had retired from Congress. Murray admitted that "the mistake of the century was the attempt to make the ex-slave

---

[18] Washington, *op. cit.*, II, 28.

[19] Woodson, *Negro Orators and Their Orations*, p. 452. Quoted by permission of The Associated Publishers, Inc.

[20] A. A. Taylor, "Negro Congressmen a Generation Afterwards," *Journal of Negro History*, VII, 170.

[21] N. P. Andrews, "The Negro in Politics," *Journal of Negro History*, V, 421 f.

a governor, before he had learned to be governed." [22] Cheatham had learned:

It is of far greater importance to the Negro to have the respect, the confidence of his next-door neighbor than who shall be President of the United States. It is of more moment to him who shall be sheriff or member of the state legislature and city council than who shall go to Congress.[23]

The conflict of opinion both as to the group and as to individuals may be well illustrated by a specific case. Although George H. White was regarded as an incendiary politician by the whites of North Carolina, Representative Haugen of Iowa speaks highly of him. "Mr. White was a quiet and unassuming gentleman and attentive to his duties, and . . . he was a gentleman of ability and high type of character." [24]

From the data and facts examined, it seems clear that the Negroes failed to accomplish much worth while in Congress, during the period under survey. They were all race conscious and supersensitive, as was perhaps unavoidable under the circumstances. With some exceptions this resulted in a neglect of their white constituents. Further, they served to keep alive race friction, and they were used as a political football by Republicans, Northern Democrats, and even on occasions by Southern Democratic factions. The honors shown them in national conventions and in other places were for the purpose of controlling delegates and votes.

This study has attempted to prove that the Negroes who served in Congress from 1870 to 1901 were as a whole superior to those of their race who, with unfortunate results, took a contemporary part in local, county, and state government. It has been demonstrated in the introductory chapter that the

[22] D. W. Culp, *Twentieth Century Negro Literature*, p. 232. Quoted by permission of J. L. Nichols and Company, Inc.

[23] *Ibid.*, p. 61.

[24] Letter to the author from Gilbert N. Haugen, November 7, 1929.

Negroes in Congress from 1870 to 1901 were rather well equipped by education, previous political experience, and wealth, and that most of them had considerable white blood in their veins and were frequently aided by white friends. Therefore, much was expected of them as they had advantages most of their race did not have. Their lack of accomplishment was an argument that the Negro would do well, for a time at least, to forego political ambition in this realm and to confine his efforts to other vocations where he had a better chance of success.

BIBLIOGRAPHY

A. PRIMARY MATERIALS

I. MANUSCRIPTS, INTERVIEWS, LETTERS

1. *Carter G. Woodson Collection* in the Library of Congress.
2. The author had personal interviews with:
   S. A. Ashe, May, 1929.
   H. P. Cheatham, August, 1929.
   Josephus Daniels, May, 1929.
   C. B. Edwards, May, 1929.
   Whitfield McKinlay, November, 1929.
   W. T. Page, November, 1929.
   Thomas Walker, November, 1929.
   C. G. Woodson, November, 1929.
3. Letters to the author concerning individual congressmen from:
   Ethel Bellune, March 23, 1930.
   H. P. Cheatham, August 8, 1929.
   Oscar DePriest, January 10, 1930.
   Gilbert N. Haugen, November 7, 1929.
   John R. Lynch, December 14, 1928; July 21, 1939.
   Thomas E. Miller, February 22, and March 4, 1930.
   Esther Osteen, March 15, 1930.
   Emma Pregnall, November 20, 1939.
   Allen Stuart, January 14, 1930.
   N. L. Willett, January 11, 1930.
4. Letters to the author on the general subject of the Negro in Congress from:
   Frederick G. Bromberg, November 25, 1929.
   W. T. Cash, July 17, 1929.
   Charles R. Crisp, November 18, 1929.
   John A. Fairlie, June 29, 1929.

J. W. Garner, September 14, 1929.
John H. Kerr, November 1, 1929.
Marie B. Owen, November 23, 1929.
F. M. Simmons, November 23, and December 18, 1929.
Herbert L. Smith, November 18, 1929.
Francis E. Williams, January 16, 1930.
John Sharp Williams, January 17, 1930.
Dorothy Winton, July 15, 1929.
C. G. Woodson, January 2, 1930.

II. BOOKS

Blaine, James G., *Twenty Years of Congress*, 2 vols., Norwich, Conn., The Henry Bill Publishing Company, 1884.

Holland, R. S., *Letters and Diary of Laura M. Towne*, Cambridge, Mass., Riverside Press, 1912.

Langston, John M., *Freedom and Citizenship*, Washington, D. C., R. H. Darby, 1883.

————, *From A Virginia Plantation to the National Capital*, Hartford, Conn., American Publishing Company, 1894.

Lynch, John R., *Facts of Reconstruction*, New York, The Neale Publishing Co., 1913.

————, *Some Historical Errors of James Ford Rhodes*, New York, The Cornhill Publishing Company, 1922.

McClure, Alexander K., *Recollections of Half a Century*, Salem, Mass., Salem Press, 1902.

Murray, George W., *Race Ideals*, Princeton, Ind., Smith and Sons, 1914.

Pike, James S., *The Prostrate State*, New York, D. Appleton and Company, 1874.

Somers, Robert, *The Southern States Since the War, 1870-1871*, New York, The Macmillan Co., 1871.

Wallace, John, *Carpet-bag Rule in Florida*, Jacksonville, Fla., DaCost Printing & Publishing House, 1888.

Warren, H. W., *Reminiscences of a Mississippi Carpetbagger*, Worcester, Mass., Davis Press, 1914.

Washington, Booker T., *The Story of the Negro*, 2 vols., New York, Doubleday, Page and Company, 1909.

Wilson, Peter M., *Southern Exposure*, Chapel Hill, The University of North Carolina Press, 1927.

III. CONVENTION PROCEEDINGS AND PUBLIC DOCUMENTS

Biographical Congressional Directory, Washington, D. C., Government Printing Office, 1929.

Congressional Globe, 1833-1873.

Congressional Record, 1873-1939.

Negro Population in the United States, Washington, D. C., Government Printing Office, 1918.

Official Proceedings National Republican Conventions of 1868, 1872, 1876, and 1880, Minneapolis, 1903.

Official Proceedings National Republican Conventions of 1884, and 1888, Minneapolis, 1903.

Official Proceedings Republican National Convention of 1892, Minneapolis, 1892.

Official Proceedings Republican National Convention of 1896, Minneapolis, 1896.

Official Proceedings Republican National Convention of 1900, Philadelphia, 1900.

Proceedings of the Constitutional Convention of South Carolina, Charleston, Denny and Perry, 1868.

IV. NEWSPAPERS

Atlanta *New Era*, Atlanta, Ga.

Charleston *Daily Courier*, Charleston, S. C.

Charleston *News and Courier*, Charleston, S. C.

Charleston *Daily Republican*, Charleston, S. C.

Columbia *Union Herald*, Columbia, S. C.

Jackson *Clarion*, Jackson, Miss.

Jackson *Pilot*, Jackson, Miss.

Jacksonville *Daily Florida Union*, Jacksonville, Fla.

Jacksonville *New South*, Jacksonville, Fla.

Memphis *Daily Avalanche*, Memphis, Tenn.

Mobile *Register*, Mobile, Ala.

Montgomery *Alabama Journal*, Montgomery, Ala.

Natchez *Daily Democrat and Courier*, Natchez, Miss.

Natchez *Daily News and Courier*, Natchez, Miss.

National Republican, Washington, D. C.

New Orleans *Republican*, New Orleans, La.
New Orleans *Times*, New Orleans, La.
New York *Sun*, New York, N. Y.
New York *Times*, New York, N. Y.
New York *Tribune*, New York, N. Y.
Oxford *Public Ledger*, Oxford, N. C.
Philadelphia *Inquirer*, Philadelphia, Pa.
Philadelphia *Times*, Philadelphia, Pa.
Raleigh *News and Observer*, Raleigh, N. C.
Raleigh *Sentinel*, Raleigh, N. C.
Richmond *Dispatch*, Richmond, Va.
Savannah *News*, Savannah, Ga.
Savannah *Republican*, Savannah, Ga.
Tallahassee *Floridian*, Tallahassee, Fla.
Tarboro *Southerner*, Tarboro, N. C.
Union Reformer, Raleigh, N. C.
Vicksburg *Times*, Vicksburg, Miss.
Washington *Evening Star*, Washington, D. C.
Washington *Post*, Washington, D. C.

V. PERIODICALS

The Atlantic Monthly, Vol. LXXXVII, April 1, 1901.
Current History, Vol. XXX.
Journal of Negro History, Vols. V, VII.
The Nation, Vol. X, February 3, March 10, April 7, June 9, 1870.
Negro Year Book, 1921-1922, Tuskegee, Tuskegee Press, 1922.
Tribune Almanac, 1870-1901.
World Almanac, 1870-1901.

B. SECONDARY MATERIALS

I. GENERAL WORKS

Andrews, N. P., "The Negro in Politics," *Journal of Negro History*, V, 421 f.
Bowers, Claude G., *The Tragic Era*, Cambridge, Mass., Houghton Mifflin Company, 1929.
Clowes, W. Laird, *Black America*, London, Cassell and Company, 1891.

Cromwell, John W., *The Negro in American History*, Washington, D. C., American Negro Academy, 1914.

Culp, D. W., *Twentieth Century Negro Literature*, Naperville, Ill., J. L. Nichols and Company, 1902.

Dowd, Jerome, *The Negro in American Life*, New York, The Century Company, 1926.

Dunning, William Archibald, *Reconstruction Political and Economic*, American Nation Series, Vol. XXII, New York, Harper and Brothers, 1906.

Ferris, William H., *The African Abroad*, 2 vols., New Haven, Tuttle, Morehouse and Taylor Press, 1913.

Fleming, Walter L., *The Sequel of Appomattox*, Chronicles of America Series, Vol. XXXII, New Haven, The Yale University Press, 1921.

Herbert, Hilary A., *Why the Solid South*, Baltimore, Md., R. H. Woodward and Company, 1890.

Nowlin, W. F., *The Negro in American National Politics since 1868*, Boston, The Stratford Company, 1931.

Reuter, Edward B., *The Mulatto in the United States*, Boston, The Gorham Press, 1918.

Rhodes, James F., *History of the United States from the Compromise of 1850*, 8 vols., New York, The Macmillan Company, 1892-1906.

Taylor, A. A., "Negro Congressmen a Generation Afterwards," *Journal of Negro History*, VII, 127-171.

Walton, Lester A., "The Negro Comes Back to the United States Congress," *Current History*, XXX (June, 1929), 461-463.

Williams, G. W., *History of the Negro Race in America*, 2 vols., New York, G. P. Putnam's Sons, 1883.

Wood, Norman B., *The White Side of a Black Subject*, Cincinnati, W. H. Ferguson Company, 1899.

Woodson, Carter G., *History of the Negro Church*, Washington, D. C., The Associated Publishers, 1921.

———, *The Negro in Our History*, Washington, D. C., The Associated Publishers, eds. of 1922 and 1928.

II. SPECIFIC WORKS

Davis, William W., *The Civil War and Reconstruction in Florida*, London, Eng., Longmans, Green and Company, 1913.

Fleming, Walter L., *Civil War and Reconstruction in Alabama*, New York, The Columbia University Press, 1905.

- Garner, J. W., *Reconstruction in Mississippi*, New York, The Macmillan Company, 1901.

Hamilton, J. G. De R., *Reconstruction in North Carolina*, London, Eng., Longmans, Green and Company, 1914.

Morton, R. L., "The Negro in Virginia Politics," Dissertation at the University of Virginia, 1918.

Reynolds, John S., *Reconstruction in South Carolina, 1865-1877*, Columbia, S. C., State Company, 1905.

Taylor, A. A., *The Negro in South Carolina During the Reconstruction*, Washington, D. C., Association for the Study of Negro Life and History, 1924.

————, *The Negro in the Reconstruction of Virginia*, Washington, D. C., Association for the Study of Negro Life and History, 1926.

Thompson, H. T., *Ousting the Carpetbagger*, Columbia, S. C., R. L. Bryan Company, 1926.

- Wallace, Jesse T., *A History of the Negroes of Mississippi, 1865-1900*, Clinton, Miss., published privately by author, 1927.

III. BIOGRAPHICAL WORKS

Allen, Walter, *Governor Chamberlain's Administration in South Carolina*, New York, G. P. Putnam's Sons, 1888.

Barnes, William H., *The American Government. History of the Forty-third Congress*, Washington, D. C., W. H. Barnes Company, 1875.

————, *History of Congress. The Forty-first Congress of the United States*, Washington, D. C., W. H. Barnes Company, 1872.

Boris, Joseph J., *Who's Who in Colored America*, New York, 1927.

Bruce, J. E., comp., *Eminent Negro Men and Women*, Yonkers, N. Y. [Gazette Press], 1910.

Councill, W. H., *Lamp of Wisdom*, Nashville, Tenn., J. T. Haley and Company, 1898.

Dictionary of American Biography, ed. Allen Johnson and Dumas Malone, 20 vols., New York, Charles Scribner's Sons, 1929-1937.

Haynes, Mrs. E. R., *Unsung Heroes*, New York, Du Bois and Dill, 1921.

Mayes, Edward, *L. Q. C. Lamar, His Life, Times and Speeches*, Nashville, Tenn., Publishing House of the Methodist Episcopal Church, South, 1896.

Poore, Ben Perley, *The Political Register and Congressional Directory*, Boston, Houghton, Osgood Company, 1878.

Quick, W. H., *Negro Stars in All Ages*, Richmond, Va., S. B. Adkins and Company, 1898.

Richardson, Clement, *National Cyclopedia of the Colored Race*, Montgomery, Ala., National Publishing Company, 1919.

Rowe, George C., *Our Heroes*, Charleston, S. C., Walker, Evans and Cogswell Company, 1890.

Simmons, William J., *Men of Mark*, Cleveland, Rewell Publishing Company, 1891.

Souvenir Journal 35th National Emancipation Celebration, Virginia, Sept. 22, 1898.

Who's Who in America, Chicago, The A. N. Marquis Company, 1928.

Who's Who in Colored America, see Boris, J. J.

Woodson, Carter G., *Negro Orators and Their Orations*, Washington, D. C., The Associated Publishers, 1925.

Work, Monroe N., comp., "Some Negro Members of Reconstruction Conventions and Legislatures and of Congress," *Journal of Negro History*, V, 63-119.

INDEX

DATE DUE

7/3			
MAY 1 7 1972			
GAYLORD			PRINTED IN U.S.A.